# The GREATEST FOOTBALL TEAMS of ALL TIME

Editor **Justin Tejada**
Designer **Drew Dzwonkowski**
Writers **Jeremy Fuchs, Elizabeth McGarr, Sam Page**
Illustrator **Martín Laksman**
Photo Editor **Abby Nicolas**
Production Manager **Hillary Leary**
Copy Editor **Jill Jaroff**

Copyright © 2018 Time Inc. Books

Published by Liberty Street,
an imprint of Time Inc. Books,
a division of Meredith Corporation
225 Liberty Street
New York, NY 10281

ISBN: 978-1-68330-072-4
Library of Congress Control Number: 2018938167

First edition, 2018
1 QGV 18
1 3 5 7 9 8 6 4 2

We welcome your comments and
suggestions about Time Inc. Books.

Time Inc. Books
Attention: Book Editors
P.O. Box 62310
Tampa, FL 33662-2310
(800) 765-6400

timeincbooks.com

Time Inc. Books products may be
purchased for business or promotional use. For
information on bulk purchases, please contact
Christi Crowley in the Special Sales
Department at (845) 895-9858.

THE **G.O.A.T** SERIES

# TABLE OF Contents

**RIDING HIGH**
The trophy presented
to the Super Bowl
champion is named
after Hall of Fame coach
Vince Lombardi, who won
five NFL championships.

# IN SEARCH OF
# GREATNESS

There are some things that unite sports fans no matter where they live, what sport they love, or which team they support.

Sports fans share a nearly universal love of all things nachos (mmm, cheese). They are among the few who believe that face paint is an acceptable fashion choice for any occasion (mm-mmm, face paint). But if there is one thing that can really bring sports fans together and ignite their passions, it is an argument about which team or player is the greatest ever.

This is especially true with football. Try gathering a group of football fans who have never met each other before and asking them one question: "Who is the greatest NFL player of all time?" You could come back five hours later, and they would still be discussing the pros and cons of different players.

Debating is one of the highlights of being a football fan. The player you think is best might not be your sister's, dad's, or grandfather's favorite. Every fan sees the game in their own way. Some value defense over offense, or passing over rushing. Those differences, and arguing about them (over nachos, of course), is part of what makes football so special.

There is a nickname for those incredible football teams and players that seem to come up in every conversation: G.O.A.T. No, we're not talking about the curious horned creatures you find on a farm. G.O.A.T. stands for Greatest Of All Time. And achieving G.O.A.T. status is what every football player aspires to.

This book is full of G.O.A.T.'s. We watched the games, reviewed the stats, and listened to the players and coaches to determine which teams and players were the greatest ever. It wasn't easy. We had plenty of debates among ourselves about these rankings. And we don't expect you to agree with all of our choices. But hopefully you will learn more about the game and be better prepared the next time a football discussion takes place. Because the only thing better than watching football is arguing about it afterward.

# CHAPTER 1

# The TOP 20 SINGLE-SEASON NFL T

The NFL has many great teams, but these rise above the rest

EAMS

# #1

## 1985 *Chicago*
# BEARS

**MAC ATTACK**
Brash quarterback Jim McMahon (9) once threw TD passes on his first two plays of a game.

hicago coach Mike Ditka noticed the substitution. And he remembered.

With his Bears being shut out in the 1984 NFC championship game, the hard-nosed and explosive Ditka watched as the San Francisco 49ers put in offensive lineman Guy McIntyre at fullback, just to add insult to injury as the clock ran out on the Bears' season.

When Chicago returned to Candlestick Park during Week 6 of the 1985 season, the Bears were 5–0 and the 49ers 3–2. Ditka got his revenge, putting his own big man, 335-pound rookie defensive lineman William (the Refrigerator) Perry, in the backfield. Fridge rushed the ball twice for four total yards. The Bears won 26–10 and made a statement: They were not just going to beat opponents—they were going to physically dominate them.

The 1985 Bears were, like the huge-but-quick Perry, a contradiction. They relished their blue-collar identity but recorded a glitzy music video for "The Super Bowl Shuffle" months before they made it to the big game. Like a 300-pound man running with a football, they were fun to watch and nearly impossible to stop.

**COACH**
Mike Ditka

**RECORD**
15–1

**SUPER BOWL XX CHAMPIONS**

## STATS INCREDIBLE!

# 7.4

**Points per game**
allowed by the Bears
at Soldier Field in
10 games that season.

## PLAYBOOK INSIDER

Linebacker **Mike Singletary**'s uncanny knowledge of opposing offenses was a signature feature of Chicago's 46 defense. On a crucial third-and-one during the NFC championship game, the Rams opened up the left side for star running back Eric Dickerson. Singletary, anticipating the play, hit the hole faster than Dickerson, forcing the Rams to punt and setting the tone for the game.

## HUT, HUT, WHAT??

During the season, quarterback **Jim McMahon** wore a headband with the Adidas logo on it. When the league fined the Bears for uniform violations, McMahon switched to a headband that read ROZELLE to poke fun at NFL commissioner Pete Rozelle.

## THE PUNKY QB

Chicago remained undefeated going into that game against the Niners thanks to two dramatic second-half comebacks engineered by quarterback Jim McMahon. In one game, against the Minnesota Vikings in Week 3, McMahon sat out the first half with back spasms and a leg infection. After pestering Ditka to let him sub in, McMahon threw touchdown passes on his first two plays of the game and added a third before the quarter ended.

The game perfectly summed up McMahon, a fourth-year quarterback out of Brigham Young University. "The Punky QB" never let injuries,

or anything else, prevent him from playing in his reckless, sporadically brilliant, style. McMahon, and the rest of the Bears' offense, were balanced by legendary running back Walter Payton. In 1985, his 11th NFL season, Payton rushed for 1,551 yards and nine touchdowns.

## THE BIG 4-6

However, it was the Bears' defense, not their offense, that made them one of the greatest teams of all time.

Led by defensive coordinator Buddy Ryan, Chicago used a signature "46 defense," with eight men in the box and just one safety back. The Bears' front eight in 1985

**SO SWEET**
In his 11th NFL season, veteran running back Walter (Sweetness) Payton (34) rushed for 1,551 yards, the third-best in the league.

"

# NO MATTER WHAT HAPPENS TOMORROW, YOU GUYS WILL ALWAYS BE MY HEROES."

—BEARS DEFENSIVE COORDINATOR **BUDDY RYAN** TO HIS PLAYERS BEFORE THE SUPER BOWL

included three future Hall of Famers: defensive linemen Richard Dent and Dan Hampton, and linebacker Mike Singletary. Chicago's defense led the NFL in yards allowed (4,135) and interceptions (34), and ranked third in sacks (64). During a three-game stretch in November, the Bears' defense actually outscored the opposing offenses.

After finishing the regular season 15–1, the Bears achieved something no team has done before or since: They posted consecutive shutouts in the playoffs, first against the New York Giants and then against the Los Angeles Rams.

Those wins propelled the Bears to the Super Bowl, fulfilling a promise Ditka had made to his players when he first took the Chicago head coaching job in 1982.

In Super Bowl XX, against the New England Patriots, the Pats focused on slowing down Walter Payton. They did that but not much else. By the third quarter, New England had negative yards on offense. The Bears sacked two different Patriots quarterbacks a total of seven times and won in dominating fashion, 46–10. To add insult to injury, Fridge even scored a rushing touchdown.

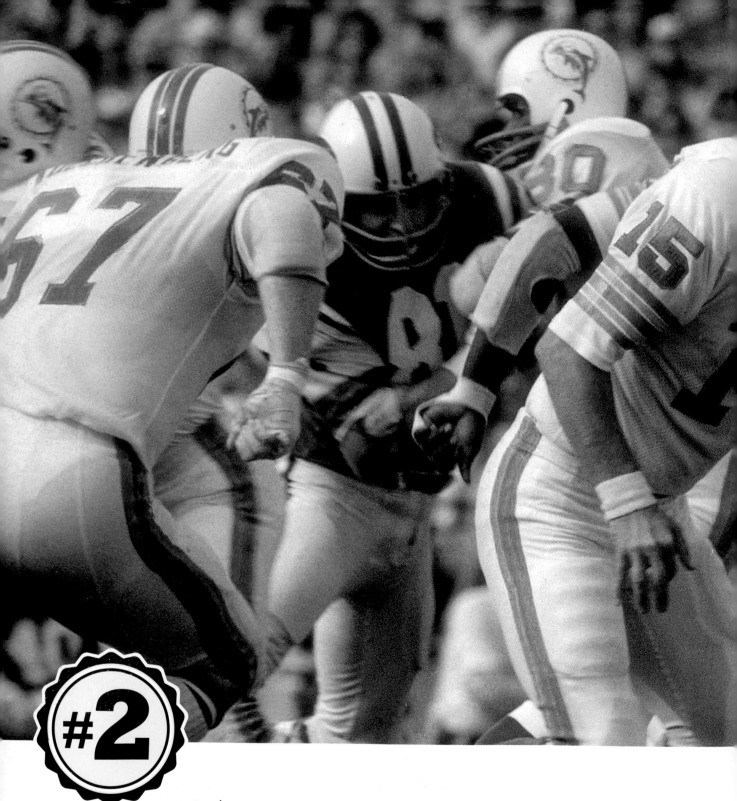

# #2

**1972** *Miami*

# DOLPHINS

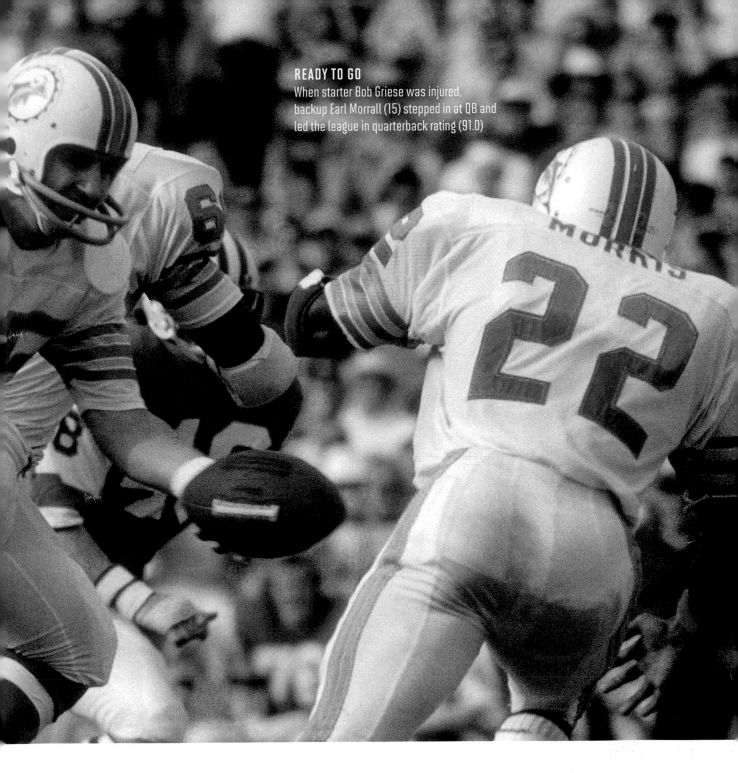

**READY TO GO**
When starter Bob Griese was injured,
backup Earl Morrall (15) stepped in at QB and
led the league in quarterback rating (91.0)

**COACH**
Don
Shula

**RECORD**
14–0

**SUPER BOWL VII
CHAMPIONS**

It's one of football's greatest urban legends: Every year, when the NFL's last remaining undefeated team suffers its first loss, the members of the 1972 Dolphins get together to share a toast.

The tale has been debunked over the years (most of the players live nowhere near each other), but it serves as an enduring reminder that there has been only one perfect team in the Super Bowl era. The Dolphins went 14–0 during the 1972 regular season, then won three straight in the playoffs, including Super Bowl VII.

The NFL's only perfect season actually started with a loss. The previous season, in Super Bowl VI, the Dallas Cowboys crushed the Dolphins 24–3. It was a bitter end to coach Don Shula's second year in Miami. The play-caller had changed the Dolphins' culture with intense practices and long meetings. But after getting blown out in the big game,

Shula returned to training camp later that year even more driven. He told his team its new goal was to go undefeated.

## CLOSE CALL

The Dolphins, however, almost took an L in Week 3. Playing the Minnesota Vikings, the Dolphins fell behind 14–6 in the fourth quarter. But a 51-yard field goal from Miami kicker Garo Yepremian made it a

> ## THEY'RE LIKE SWARMING BEES. YOU THINK YOU'VE BLOCKED THEM WELL, AND YOU ONLY GET TWO, THREE, FOUR YARDS BEFORE THEY'RE ALL OVER YOU."
>
> —WASHINGTON GUARD **JOHN WILBUR**, ON THE MIAMI DEFENSE

one-possession game. Dolphins quarterback Bob Griese led a two-minute drill and marched his team to the Vikings' three-yard line. There, Griese faked a handoff to fullback Larry Csonka to execute a perfect play-action touchdown pass to tight end Jim Mandich that gave Miami the win.

Opposing defenses had to respect

**BOWLED OVER**
Fullback Larry Csonka (39) was one of the game's best power rushers. He gained 112 yards on 15 carries in Super Bowl VII.

## UNSUNG HERO

Running back **Jim Kiick** had been Csonka's partner in crime but lost touches in 1972 to Mercury Morris. Kiick took the demotion in stride and became a great third-down back for the team. During Miami's playoff run, he scored four touchdowns.

## STATS INCREDIBLE!

# 170

Rushing first downs by the 1972 Dolphins, 25 more than the next-best team, the Oakland Raiders.

## HUT, HUT, WHAT??

Defensive tackle Manny Fernandez and fullback Larry Csonka pulled a mean prank on Don Shula when they put a **three-foot alligator** in their coach's shower. They had caught the reptile while fishing and were nice enough (to the coach!) to tape its mouth shut first.

Csonka. In an era when fullbacks still ran the ball, he was one of the best. At 6' 3" and more than 230 pounds, Csonka bowled over defenders. He was joined in the backfield in 1972 by running back Mercury Morris. He and Csonka formed one of the great speed-power duos, each rushing for at least 1,000 yards.

Even a season-ending leg injury to star quarterback Bob Griese in the fifth game of the season couldn't derail the Dolphins. Thirty-eight-year-old backup Earl Morrall stepped in and never looked back. Morrall went 9–0 and led the league with a 91.0 quarterback rating.

## NO-NAMES NO MORE

In addition to the league's top-ranked offense, the Dolphins' defense also allowed the fewest yards of any team in 1972. The so-called No-Name Defense—a nickname given by Cowboys coach Tom Landry—produced just one Hall of Famer, Nick Buoniconti, but it dominated through team effort and attention to detail.

With an unstoppable running attack and tough defense, the Dolphins advanced to Super Bowl VII against the Washington Redskins. Washington running back Larry Brown led the league in yards per game during the regular season but was ineffective against a Dolphins D featuring defensive tackle Manny Fernandez, who finished with 17 tackles. Meanwhile, Csonka ran for 112 yards on just 15 carries.

The Dolphins almost finished their 17–0 season with a 17–0 score. But Washington blocked the Miami field goal that would have made it 17–0 and returned it for a touchdown. The final score was 14–7. Even without that cherry on top, nothing could take away from what the Dolphins had achieved: perfection.

# #3

## 2007 *New England* PATRIOTS

**COACH**
Bill Belichick

**RECORD**
16-0

**AFC CHAMPIONS**

We know what you're thinking: the 2007 Patriots, a team most famous for losing the Super Bowl? How can they be the third-greatest team of all time?

Well, maybe—just maybe—winning the Super Bowl isn't everything. In fact, if all the teams in our Top 20 faced off in a tournament, the 2007 Patriots might just be the favorites to win out.

The Pats' passing attack was basically unstoppable. One of the greatest quarterbacks ever, Tom Brady, combined with one of the greatest wide receivers ever, Randy Moss, to set the NFL single-season records for passing touchdowns (50) and receiving touchdowns (23).

Moss was already an NFL legend by 2007. But the season before, in

**ALMOST PERFECT**
Tom Brady (12)
broke the NFL
single-season record
for touchdown
passes in 2007,
with 50.

**A NEW MAN**
After catching 67 passes with Miami in 2006, Wes Welker (83) tied for the NFL lead with 112 receptions after joining the Pats in 2007.

## PLAYBOOK INSIDER

In Week 17, with their perfect season on the line, the Patriots trailed the Giants 23–28 in the fourth quarter. On his own 35, Tom Brady threw a deep arcing pass to **Randy Moss**, who outran his defender down the field. The ensuing touchdown simultaneously gave Brady and Moss single-season touchdown records at their positions.

## STATS INCREDIBLE!

# 47.0
Total sacks by the Patriots' defense, second in the league, which proved New England wasn't just an offensive juggernaut.

## UNSUNG HERO

The addition of **Donté Stallworth** might not have generated the same attention as Welker and Moss. But Stallworth's 697 yards gave Brady a reliable third option and kept teams from becoming too focused on any one target.

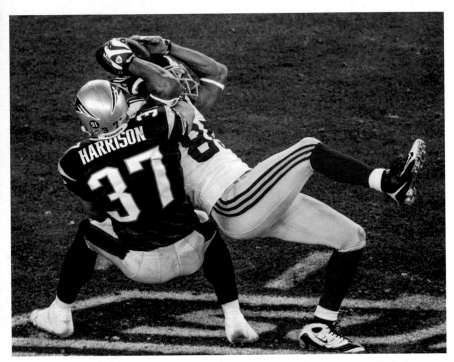

**CATCHING A MIRACLE** New York Giants receiver David Tyree caught a ball on his helmet to set up the score that ended the Patriots' perfect season.

Oakland, he had caught a career-low 42 passes. Patriots coach Bill Belichick, who has a habit of getting the most out of players at every stage of their careers, was able to snatch up Moss in exchange for just a fourth-round draft pick.

Moss wasn't the only important wideout New England acquired before the 2007 season. Receiver and kick returner Wes Welker, another player Belichick coveted, came over from the Miami Dolphins in exchange for second- and seventh-round picks.

## NEW BEGINNINGS

Welker and Moss were coming off a 2006 season in which they had a total of 1,240 receiving yards and four touchdowns. A year later, with Brady throwing passes their way, the duo combined for 2,668 yards and 31 touchdowns.

With that explosive offense, the Pats defeated each of their first eight

## THEY HAVE DISTANCED THEMSELVES FROM THE REST OF THE LEAGUE IN A WAY THAT I HAVE NOT SEEN IN 30 YEARS OF WATCHING FOOTBALL."

—JIM MANDICH, TIGHT END ON THE UNDEFEATED 1972 DOLPHINS

opponents by double-digit margins. New England set a regular-season record with a point differential of 315. In other words, the Patriots averaged nearly a three-touchdown lead in all their regular-season games.

That doesn't mean it was easy. In Weeks 12 and 13, against the Philadelphia Eagles and the Baltimore Ravens, respectively, the Pats needed Brady to lead fourth-quarter comebacks to win. In Week 17, the Pats trailed the New York Giants 28–16 late in the third quarter before rallying to win 38–35.

Then, of course, there was SpyGate, an incident in which the Patriots were caught videotaping New York Jets coaches' signals from the sidelines. The league fined Belichick the maximum of $500,000.

## ALMOST PERFECT

Still, the Patriots entered Super Bowl XLII undefeated. In a rematch of the regular-season finale against the Giants, Brady led the Patriots to a 14–10 lead with less than three minutes to go.

It seemed it would take a miracle to defeat the Patriots. And that's just what happened. The Giants drove down the field, and after a miraculous catch in which David Tyree pinned the ball to his helmet, they scored the winning touchdown. The Patriots were stunned.

"Guys forgot what it was like to lose a game," Pats wide receiver Donté Stallworth said afterward.

Even the defeat can't diminish what the Patriots accomplished. New England went 18–0 before that Super Bowl, the longest unbeaten stretch by any team on this list. (The undefeated 1972 Dolphins only played a 14-game regular season.)

Still it's hard not to wonder what could have been. Had the Patriots blown their Week 17 matchup with the Giants instead of the Super Bowl, they would likely eclipse another 18–1 team, the 1985 Chicago Bears, as the consensus G.O.A.T.

# #4

## 1962 *Green Bay* PACKERS

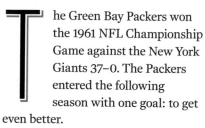

**COACH**
Vince
Lombardi

---

**RECORD**
13–1

---

**1962 NFL
CHAMPIONS**

The Green Bay Packers won the 1961 NFL Championship Game against the New York Giants 37–0. The Packers entered the following season with one goal: to get even better.

Green Bay started the 1962 season by winning its first three games by a combined margin of 100–7. The hot start included back-to-back shutouts of the St. Louis Cardinals and the Chicago Bears. The Pack's 49–0 victory over the Bears was one of two seven-touchdown victories they would have that season.

Packers Hall of Fame coach Vince Lombardi overwhelmed his competition with a smashmouth running attack the likes of which has never been matched in the NFL. In only a 14-game season, fullback Jim Taylor rushed for 1,474 yards and 19 touchdowns. Green Bay's

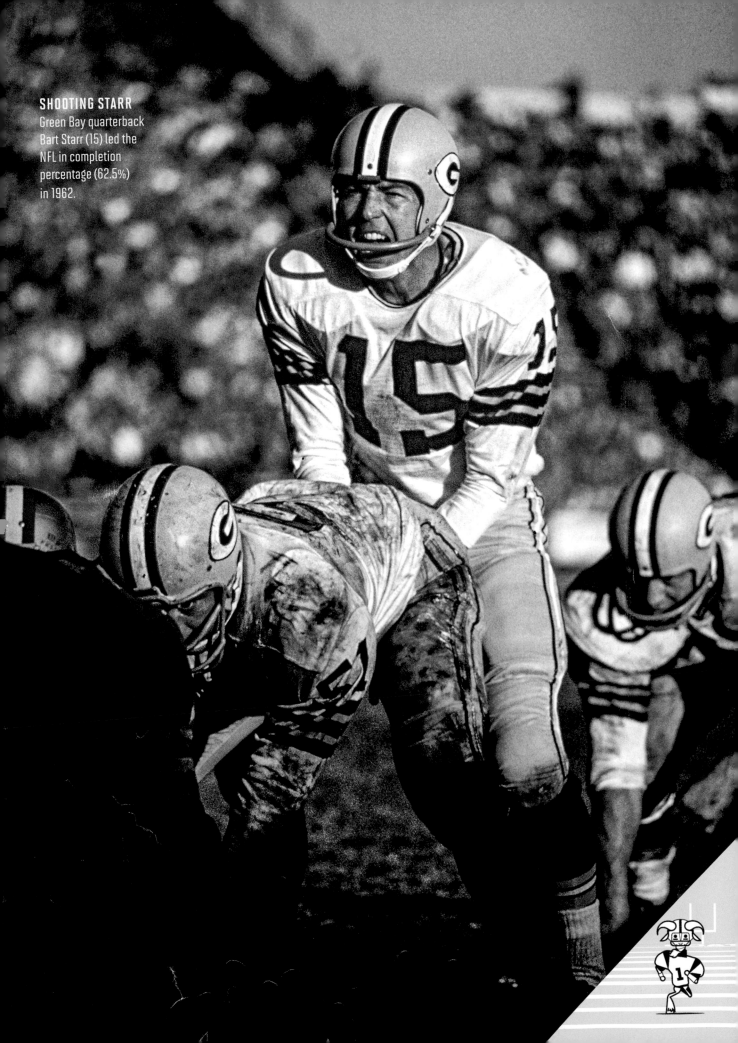

**SHOOTING STARR**
Green Bay quarterback Bart Starr (15) led the NFL in completion percentage (62.5%) in 1962.

## UNSUNG HERO

**Buyd Dowler's** contributions to the 1962 Packers weren't limited to one position. As a flanker—a wide receiver that lines up behind the line of scrimmage—Dowler had 724 yards receiving. As a punter, he averaged 43.1 yards per kick.

## STATS INCREDIBLE!

# 574

**More yards of offense** the Packers gained than the Philadelphia Eagles in Week 9. In a 49–0 blowout, Green Bay had 628 yards of total offense compared with Philadelphia's 54.

## HUT, HUT, WHAT??

After winning MVP of the 1962 NFL Championship Game, Packers linebacker **Ray Nitschke** appeared that same night on the popular game show *What's My Line?* in which the panelists tried to guess his line of work through a series of questions.

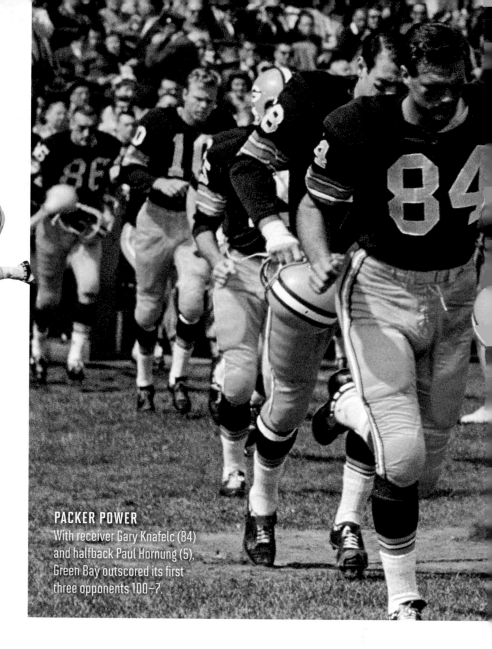

**PACKER POWER**
With receiver Gary Knafelc (84) and halfback Paul Hornung (5), Green Bay outscored its first three opponents 100–7.

36 total rushing touchdowns in 1962 still stand as an NFL single-season record.

The Packers dominated every aspect of the game. Quarterback Bart Starr completed 62.5% of his passes in an era when anything over 60% seemed impossible. Green Bay's defense allowed just 10 passing touchdowns all season, the fewest in the league. It also led the NFL in interceptions with 31.

In Week 10, the Baltimore Colts managed to hold Taylor to 46 yards rushing and Starr to 57 yards passing. But Green Bay's Herb Adderley scored on a 103-yard kick-return touchdown and intercepted Johnny Unitas at a key moment to help the Packers win their 10th game in a row, 17–13.

## TALENT TO SPARE

The Colts game showed that, even in the rare instance in which they were outplayed, the Packers seemed to have too much talent to lose. The roster of the 1962 Packers was truly stacked. It featured 10 All-Pro players, nine Pro Bowlers, and 10 future Hall of Famers.

Perhaps the most enduring symbol of Green Bay's greatness was that the

> ## "
> ## WE'LL SHOW THEM. WE'RE TIRED OF READING ABOUT HOW THEY HAD AN OFF DAY AGAINST US. I HOPE THEY HAVE A REAL GOOD DAY TODAY."
>
> —PACKERS SAFETY
> **HANK GREMMINGER** BEFORE
> THE NFL CHAMPIONSHIP GAME

team's one loss—in Week 11 against Detroit—was so hard to believe that it earned its own nickname, the Thanksgiving Day Massacre. And the final score wasn't even that bad (26–14).

The Packers made up for their loss by winning the final three games of the regular season on their way to a championship game rematch with the Giants in Yankee Stadium. New York wanted to prove to its home fans that the previous year's blowout had been a fluke. Green Bay welcomed the challenge.

The Giants played well. It wasn't

enough. After a blocked punt return for a touchdown helped the Giants shrink Green Bay's lead to 10–7, New York failed to get its passing attack going. Meanwhile, the Packers ran the ball well late in the fourth quarter, setting up a pair of game-icing field goals that secured a 16–7 victory.

Green Bay would go on to win three more NFL titles and the first two Super Bowls under Lombardi. But even among those great teams, the dominance of the 1962 squad stands alone.

# #5

## 1989 *San Francisco*
# 49ERS

Before the start of the 1989 NFL season, the unthinkable happened: Bill Walsh retired. After winning Super Bowl XXIII against the Cincinnati Bengals, the San Francisco 49ers' legendary coach immediately stepped down.

It was hard to imagine the Niners without Walsh. Starting as an assistant coach in Cincinnati, Walsh had innovated the West Coast offense, which prioritized short throws over long bombs. In San Francisco, Walsh had the pieces he needed to perfect the system with quarterback Joe Montana and wideout Jerry Rice. By 1989, Walsh had already led San Francisco to three Super Bowl titles.

George Seifert, Walsh's defensive coordinator, took over as head coach. Seifert was a San Francisco native and longtime 49ers fan who had made his way up the ranks for his hometown

**COACH**
George Seifert

**RECORD**
14–2

**SUPER BOWL XXIV CHAMPIONS**

team. He had spent most of his time coaching from the press box. Now, as head coach, he stood on the sideline, where fans and players noticed his quirks and superstitions, like never stepping on the 49ers logo at midfield.

Whatever Seifert was doing, it was working. He won his first two games as head coach. Then at home against the Philadelphia Eagles in Week 3, the 49ers had a signature win. Trailing 21–10, Montana threw four touchdown passes in the fourth quarter. San Francisco won 38–28. Joe Cool had once again proved to be unfazed by pressure.

Under offensive coordinator Mike Holmgren, the 49ers led the NFL in total yards (6,268) and passing touchdowns (35) in 1989. Rice and John Taylor were the league's premier receiving duo, with each player nabbing at least 1,000 yards and 10 touchdowns. Montana's secret

**COOL AS ICE**
Niners quarterback
Joe Montana (16) earned
the nickname Joe Cool
for his clutch play.

weapon was fullback Tom Rathman, who rushed for 305 yards but also had 616 yards receiving out of the backfield.

At times, the offense seemed so good, it didn't matter who ran it. Future Hall of Famer Steve Young had a perfect 158.3 passer rating in relief of an injured Montana in Week 7 against the New England Patriots. When Young went out with an injury in the next game, against the

> ## YOU LOOK AT [MONTANA] FROM THE SIDELINES, AND YOU'RE ALMOST IN AWE. YOU FIND YOURSELF WATCHING LIKE A FAN WOULD."
>
> —49ERS COACH **GEORGE SEIFERT**

New York Jets, third-stringer Steve Bono stepped in to complete four of five passes, including a touchdown.

## JOE COOL AND THE GANG

That incredible depth delivered the Niners to a 14–2 regular-season finish. Their success, however, did little to prepare the rest of the league for the playoff dominance to come.

San Francisco drew the Minnesota Vikings, the league's Number 1–ranked defense, in the divisional round. The Vikings had nearly tied the NFL sack record (72) during the regular season

## LEADER OF THE HERD

While Montana captained the offense, the undisputed leader of the defense was **Ronnie Lott**. The safety had played on all three of Walsh's championship-winning teams and maintained his hard-hitting style after Seifert took over. "There was something special about him that his spirit kind of permeated through the rest of that club," Seifert would tell NFL Network.

## HUT, HUT, WHAT??

Coach George Seifert had a number of superstitions, such as refusing to step on the 49ers logo at the 50-yard line. But one of the weirdest was Seifert's insistence on blowing on a **breath mint** three times before every game.

## UNSUNG HERO

Though the Niners' offense was best known for the Montana-Rice connection, running back **Roger Craig** rushed for 1,054 yards of his own on 271 carries in 1989. A year removed from leading the league with 2,036 yards from scrimmage, Craig also gave Montana yet another short-yardage option in the passing game.

but didn't get Montana once during the game. Minnesota loved to use stunts, in which defensive players switched pass-rushing lanes, to confuse offensive lines all season. The Niners' front five, however, focused on blocking areas instead of men.

It also helped that Montana needed only a few seconds to find Rice or Taylor on a quick slant. In the box score, it looked as if Joe Cool was hitting them for deep strikes, but the routes were short. The West Coast offense was built to help receivers pick up big yardage after the catch. Rice scored his team's first touchdown on a 72-yard reception. But he had caught the ball right in front of the line of scrimmage. The Niners shredded the Vikings' vaunted D 41–13.

In the NFC championship game against the L.A. Rams, Seifert's defense stepped up. They hit Rams QB Jim Everett so often, he went down on his own late in the game for a "phantom sack." The Niners won another blowout, 30–3.

Super Bowl XXIV was a showdown between two very different legends under center. While Montana brilliantly executed the methodical West Coast offense, Denver's John Elway did his best work when plays broke down. He would scramble out of the pocket and find a streaking receiver with a deep throw. This time, however, order won out over chaos. The 49ers embarrassed yet another of the league's top defenses, this time 55–10.

In total, San Francisco outscored its opponents by 100 points during the 1989 playoffs (126–26). And while the 49ers would fail to pull off the NFL's first "three-peat" the following season, that takes nothing away from the brilliance of the 1989 team.

# #6

**1991** *Washington*
# REDSKINS

**HOG WILD** Playing behind a strong offensive line, quarterback Mark Rypien (11) helped the Skins lead the NFL in yards per pass attempt (8.1).

**COACH**
Joe
Gibbs

**RECORD**
14–2

**SUPER BOWL XXVI CHAMPIONS**

From 1982 through 1991, the Washington Redskins won three Super Bowls. But for some reason Washington is not often included on lists of the NFL's great dynasties.

Maybe the Redskins never get their due because of what was unique about each team: A different quarterback won each Super Bowl. Or maybe they fly under the radar because of what they had in common: a dominant offensive line and an unassuming head coach. Nevertheless, the 1991 Washington Redskins were something special.

That offensive line at least had a memorable nickname—the Hogs—coined by Washington O-line coach Joe Bugel in 1982. By 1991, two of the original Hogs were still oinking on the Washington line: center Jeff Bostic and tackle Joe Jacoby. The holes Jacoby opened up on the right side of the line helped Skins running back Earnest Byner rush for 1,048 yards that season, fifth-best in the NFL.

Washington head coach Joe Gibbs was so devoted to football that he became famous for sleeping at the Redskins' practice complex. Gibbs certainly had his hands full in planning the 1991 team's attack. The season before, third-year quarterback Mark Rypien played poorly, blowing the team's divisional round playoff game against the San Francisco 49ers with three interceptions. Rypien held out for a new contract during the preseason and didn't look particularly sharp when he finally did report at the start of 1991.

## LET 'ER RYP

When the season got under way, however, everything immediately clicked. Rypien threw for two touchdowns in a 45–0 rout of the Detroit Lions in Week 1. He had uncanny accuracy on deep throws. All season, he would hit the Posse—receivers Gary Clark, Art Monk, and Ricky Sanders—with home run throws. The Skins averaged 8.1 yards per passing attempt—by far the most in the league.

By their Week 8 bye, Washington was 7–0 and had already shut out three opponents. Despite boasting just one All-Pro player—future Hall of Fame cornerback Darrell Green—the defense dominated. The Redskins ranked second in the league in interceptions (27) and tied for third in sacks (50). The unit was like the rest of the team: low in star power, high in production.

When the regular season ended, the Redskins were 14–2, and no one could afford to ignore them anymore. That didn't mean they felt respected. They couldn't help but notice, for instance, boxer Evander Holyfield and rapper MC Hammer on the Atlanta sideline before their first-round playoff matchup

against the Falcons. Washington gave Hammer nothing to cheer about, picking off Atlanta QB Chris Miller four times in a 24–7 win.

The next week, in the NFC championship game, the Hogs mauled the Lions. Washington rushed for 117 yards and two touchdowns and allowed zero sacks. The Skins won easily, 41–10.

Given that performance, Buffalo Bills defensive line coach Chuck Dickerson was playing with fire when he insulted the Hogs before his team played Washington in the Super Bowl. He called Jacoby a "Neanderthal" who "slobbers a lot" and Bostic "ugly like the rest of them." With two weeks to work on his notoriously thorough preparation, Gibbs made sure his team was ready for the big game. He also made sure they saw a tape of Dickerson's remarks.

Unsurprisingly, the motivated Redskins dominated in the trenches. They rushed for 125 yards and two touchdowns and once again allowed no sacks. Working from a clean pocket, Rypien showed just how far he'd come from a year before, throwing for 292 yards and two touchdowns and earning MVP honors.

Like so many players on the 1991 team, Rypien would not go on to a Hall of Fame career. But together, those Redskins were one of the NFL's greatest squads of all time—and definitely the most underrated.

> ## WE KNEW THEY WEREN'T AS CONFIDENT AS THEY ACTED. WHEN YOU TALK LIKE THAT, YOU'RE KIND OF HIDING BEHIND YOUR WORDS. BUT YOU KNOW THE REAL DEAL."
>
> —WASHINGTON DEFENSIVE END **CHARLES MANN**, ON THE FALCONS' TRASH TALK IN THE PLAYOFFS

### LEADER OF THE HERD

Defensive end **Charles Mann** led the defense with 11½ sacks, and had 63 tackles and three forced fumbles. He also earned the game ball in Week 3 when he had four tackles, two sacks, and one forced fumble just hours after the birth of his son, Cameron.

### STATS INCREDIBLE!

**7** Times that QB Mark Rypien was sacked in 1991. The NFL average for sacks allowed that season was 35.

### PLAYBOOK INSIDER

In one meeting, quarterbacks coach Rod Dowhower suggested a new play: the Sprint Bomb. Receivers would sprint down one end of the field, drawing opposing safeties away from **Gary Clark**, who would sneak down the other sideline. Washington ran the Sprint Bomb in Week 9 against the New York Giants. Rypien hit Clark in single-coverage for a 54-yard touchdown that put Washington on top for good and helped it better its record to 8–0.

**CATCH A STAR**
Art Monk (81) led a trio of receivers, along with Gary Clark and Ricky Sanders, that was nicknamed the Posse.

**MAN OF STEEL**
Pittsburgh quarterback Terry
Bradshaw (12) led the NFL with
28 touchdown passes in 1978.

# #7

## 1978 *Pittsburgh* STEELERS

**COACH**
Chuck Noll

--------

**RECORD**
14–2

--------

**SUPER BOWL XIII CHAMPIONS**

Picking the single best Pittsburgh Steelers team from their dynasty in the 1970s isn't easy. The Steelers won back-to-back Super Bowls following the 1974 and 1975 seasons. Even among that greatness, the 1978 team stands out.

In 1978, Pittsburgh quarterback Terry Bradshaw threw for 2,915 yards and an NFL-best 28 touchdowns. The receivers on the other end of most of those TD passes were a pair of future Hall of Famers, Lynn Swann and John Stallworth.

A solid ground game? Well, the Steelers had that, too, thanks to bruising back Franco Harris, another future Hall of Famer, who put together his fifth-straight 1,000-yard rushing season in 1978.

Pittsburgh's famous Steel Curtain defense was also intact that season. The Steelers had the AFC's best rushing D, holding opponents to 110.9 yards per game on the ground.

The Terrible Towel–waving fans in Pittsburgh, spoiled by two championships already, were hungry for more, and the Steelers gave them what they wanted.

## CATCHING ON

Swann received most of the attention from fans and defenses, but in the divisional playoffs against the Denver Broncos, it was Stallworth who shone when Denver double-covered Swann. Stallworth hauled in a playoff-record 10 catches for 156 yards and one touchdown. Said Swann after Pittsburgh's 33–10 victory, "About halfway through the game, I kept looking at John and saying to myself, *Hey, that's supposed to be me doing that!*"

The Steelers then ran over the Houston Oilers in the AFC title game 34–5. With Pittsburgh's trip to its third Super Bowl of the decade secure, cameras caught Swann and Stallworth celebrating together on the sideline. "We got the best offense, the best defense, the best QB, the best running back, the best everything, best coaching staff, best front office—and we got the Terrible Towel," said Swann.

**DOUBLE TROUBLE** Steelers receivers John Stallworth (left) and Lynn Swann both went on to be inducted into the Hall of Fame.

On Pittsburgh's very first defensive play of the AFC title game, linebacker **Jack Ham** stuffed Houston Oilers star running back Earl Campbell for a three-yard loss. The play set the tone for the game, which took place in sloppy conditions at Pittsburgh's Three Rivers Stadium. With rain and sleet falling and temperatures in the teens with the windchill, Ham had an interception and two fumble recoveries. In total, the Steelers forced nine turnovers on their way to a 34–5 win.

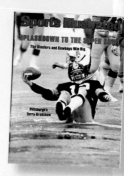

"Terrible Towel. What more do we need?" asked Stallworth.

Winning the Super Bowl was going to take more than a piece of yellow terry cloth, though. The Steelers had beaten the Cowboys in Super Bowl X, but Dallas entered Super Bowl XIII as the defending champion.

The game was one of the greatest of all time: The score was tied 7–7, then 14–14, and would have been 21–21 but for a dropped pass in the end zone by Cowboys tight end Jackie Smith.

Then, just as the Steelers expanded their lead in the fourth quarter, the Cowboys rallied. "Our guys started celebrating when it was 35–17, and it made me mad," Bradshaw said later. "The game wasn't over."

It sure wasn't. Dallas was one onside-kick recovery away from having a chance to take the lead with less than a minute to play. But Pittsburgh running back Rocky Bleier, who had already caught a touchdown that day, fell on the ball. The Steelers ran out the clock for a 35–31 win. They were the first team to win three Super Bowls—and the very next year, they won it all again.

> PLAYING PITTSBURGH IS LIKE EATING AN ICE CREAM CONE ON A HOT SUMMER DAY. SOMETIMES BEFORE YOU CAN GET IT ALL IN YOUR MOUTH, IT GETS ALL OVER YOU."
>
> —OILERS COACH **BUM PHILLIPS**, BEFORE THE 1978 AFC TITLE GAME

The Steelers' D earned its nickname in 1971, when a local radio station held a contest to name the ferocious unit. Greg Kronz, a ninth-grader at Montour High School outside Pittsburgh, submitted the nickname **Steel Curtain**, and he won! The nickname was inspired by the Cold War–era Iron Curtain.

# 8.7

Points per game allowed by the Steelers in their seven consecutive wins leading up to Super Bowl XIII.

**SWANN SONG**
Lynn Swann (88) had 124 receiving yards and a touchdown in Super Bowl XIII against the Dallas Cowboys.

**HOW BOUT 'DEM COWBOYS?**
In 1992, Troy Aikman (8) completed a playoff
record 89 passes without an interception.

# #8

**1992** *Dallas*

# COWBOYS

After the Dallas Cowboys dominated in 1992, it was easy to forget that the team was just three years removed from a 1–15 finish. The Cowboys came into 1992 fresh off their first postseason appearance in six years. Despite a loss in the 1991 divisional round to the Detroit Lions, the players and fourth-year coach Jimmy Johnson knew they had something special.

The 1992 Cowboys won three games to start the season for the first time since 1983. They went on to clinch the NFC East title for the first time since 1985.

Dallas's young defense was energized by the addition of All-Pro defensive end Charles Haley. It became the league's top unit (254.6 yards allowed per game). But teams still underestimated Dallas all season.

"The Eagles, the Giants, the Redskins—they all came out figuring they could pound us," said Cowboys

**COACH**
Jimmy
Johnson

**RECORD**
13–3

**SUPER
BOWL XXVII
CHAMPIONS**

tight end Alfredo Roberts when the team was 8–1. "Everyone figures that. I don't know why."

Fourth-year quarterback Troy Aikman led the charge for the NFC's second-ranked offense. He found Pro Bowl wide receiver Michael Irvin 78 times for 1,396 yards. The Cowboys

# AN EARTHQUAKE IN SANTA MONICA TONIGHT... THAT'S THE ONLY THING THAT CAN STOP THE COWBOYS."

—BUFFALO WIDE RECEIVER **JAMES LOFTON**, AFTER SUPER BOWL XXVII

balanced their passing game with a spectacular rushing attack. Third-year running back Emmitt Smith ran for 1,713 yards on his way to a second-straight NFL rushing title.

## ROSY FUTURE

In the playoffs, the Cowboys beat the divisional rival Philadelphia Eagles for the second time that season. They limited Philly QB Randall Cunningham to 160 yards through the air and won 34–10. "Every time I saw somebody open for a second, the Cowboys were back in my face," said Cunningham.

The NFC championship game was a showdown between the conference's top two offenses: Dallas and the

**SLAM DUNK**
Receiver Alvin Harper's (80) touchdown helped the Cowboys pile on 52 points in Super Bowl XXVII.

## LEADER OF THE HERD

**Troy Aikman** was named MVP of Super Bowl XXVII after throwing for 273 yards and four touchdowns. When the game against the Bills ended, he had completed 89 passes without an interception, setting a new playoff record.

## HUT, HUT, WHAT??

Leon Lett was a goat of a different sort in Super Bowl XXVII. Showboating on the way to the end zone during a 64-yard fumble return (the Cowboys led 52–17 at this point), Lett held the ball away from his body. Bills receiver Don Beebe, who had sprinted 90 yards downfield, **knocked it away**, preventing an easy touchdown.

## UNSUNG HERO

Running back Emmitt Smith was the superstar, but it was fullback **Daryl (Moose) Johnston** who paved the way for the NFL's rushing leader. Johnston also carried the ball on occasion, much to the delight of the fans in Dallas, who would yell, "Moooooose!" whenever he touched the pigskin.

San Francisco 49ers. Tied 10–10 at halftime, the Cowboys pulled ahead slightly in the second half. But in control of the ball with 4:22 left, they were only up 24–20. On first down, the 49ers came on the blitz; instead of passing to Irvin, his playmaker, Aikman found wideout Alvin Harper, who caught the ball at the Dallas 35 and ran all the way down to the 49ers' nine-yard line. Aikman then connected with Kelvin Martin in the end zone, clinching a 30–20 victory.

"How 'bout them Cowboys?!" Johnson shouted to his jubilant players in the locker room afterward. His team was now headed to Super Bowl XXVII in Pasadena, California, where they would face the Buffalo Bills.

Many thought the Bills, who had lost the previous two Super Bowls, would finally win a title. Third time's the charm, right?

Nope. Not even close. Buffalo QB Jim Kelly left the game with an injury in the second quarter. He and backup Frank Reich each threw two interceptions. (Reich also had three fumbles.) The Cowboys rolled to a 52–17 victory at the Rose Bowl stadium.

"You never in a million years think about scoring 52 points," said Dallas offensive coordinator Norv Turner. "But they turned the ball over nine times, so that's what can happen."

After the game, sportswriters used the word "dynasty" over and over again. They were right. The Cowboys would repeat as champions the next year (beating the poor Bills again) and went on two years later to win Super Bowl XXX as well.

Said Dallas defensive end Jim Jeffcoat after that Super Bowl XXVII victory, "We're now on top of the world, and we're not coming off."

**#9**

1996 *Green Bay*
# PACKERS

**COACH**
Mike
Holmgren

**RECORD**
13–3

**SUPER BOWL XXXI
CHAMPIONS**

The Packers won the first two Super Bowls ever played, in the 1960s. They didn't return to the big game until its 31st edition. It took Brett Favre to lead them there.

When Favre began his career with the Packers, the quarterback did not look as if he would win three MVP awards. A scrambler who wasn't very good at improvising after the snap, Favre struggled with accuracy and handling the playbook after becoming the starting QB in 1992.

But in 1993 he led Green Bay to the playoffs after a 10-season drought. In 1995 he won his first MVP award and took the Packers all the way to the NFC championship game, but they lost to the Dallas Cowboys.

The 38–27 defeat left a bitter taste in Green Bay players' mouths. On the team flight home from Dallas, Favre, defensive star Reggie White, and other

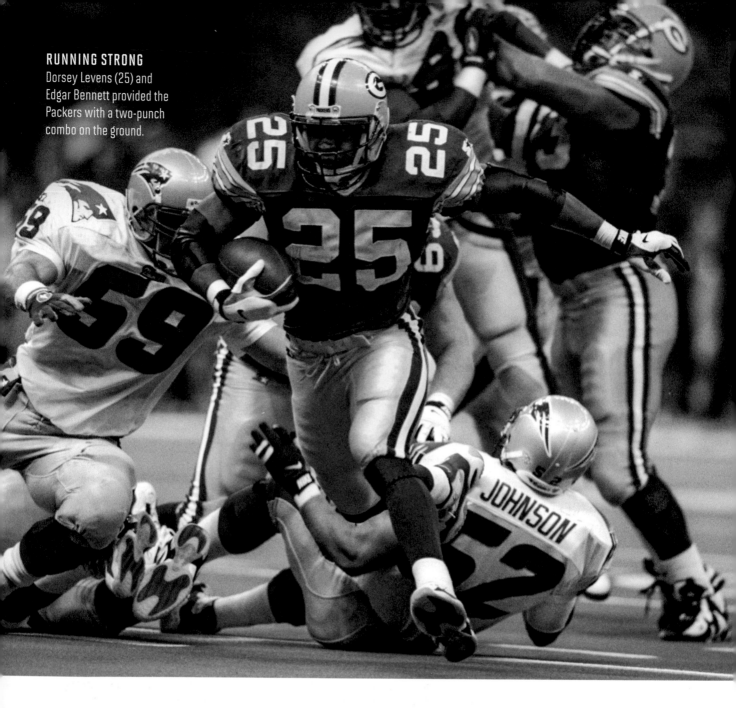

**RUNNING STRONG**
Dorsey Levens (25) and Edgar Bennett provided the Packers with a two-punch combo on the ground.

## STATS INCREDIBLE!

# 19

**Touchdowns allowed** by the Green Bay Packers in 1996. The total was the fewest since the NFL went to a 16-game season in 1978. Only the 2000 Ravens have ever allowed fewer (18).

## HUT, HUT, WHAT??

The **Lambeau Leap** really took off in 1996. Receiver Robert Brooks jumped into the stands after scoring in a 1995 game, and his teammates got in on the action the following season. "The first time I did it and saw the TV highlights, I thought, Man, that is so much fun! It's just the best," Brooks said.

## LEADER OF THE HERD

In 1996, defensive end **Reggie White** made his 11th-straight Pro Bowl. Known as the Minister of Defense (he was also a preacher), White was the team's emotional leader. He led the Pack in sacks until his last season with the team, in 1998.

## THIS TEAM HAS BEEN KIND OF LIKE POTLUCK, A MIXTURE OF THE GOOD, THE BAD, AND THE UGLY."

—QUARTERBACK **BRETT FAVRE**, AFTER THE NFC CHAMPIONSHIP GAME, 1996–1997 SEASON

veterans made a promise. If they ever made it to the conference title game again, they were going to make it to the Super Bowl.

In 1996, Favre set a team record with a league-best 39 touchdown passes. The Packers won 13 games and secured home field advantage in the playoffs.

### MANY HAPPY RETURNS

The Packers' Lambeau Field in January can be, to put it mildly, chilly. But for the divisional playoff game against the 49ers, the weather was a relatively warm 24° with the windchill. In the game's first eight minutes, the Packers went up 14–0. Return specialist Desmond Howard took one punt 71 yards for a touchdown and another 41 yards that set up a second score. Green Bay didn't look back. The team's 35–14 win meant the Packers were indeed back in the NFC title game—this time against the Carolina Panthers.

For that game, the temperature was a more Green Bay–like –25° with the windchill. Favre started slow, throwing a first-quarter interception that led to a Carolina touchdown. "I was overthinking," he said, "worrying too much about what they were doing." He settled into a groove, throwing for 292 yards and two touchdowns.

The running game got plenty of action, too, with Edgar Bennett and Dorsey Levens averaging 5.3 yards per carry against a defense that had allowed only 4.2 during the regular season. "The whole story was them running the ball," Panthers cornerback Toi Cook said afterward. "I never thought I'd see the day when they'd just run all over us."

A 30–13 victory sent the Packers to Super Bowl XXXI in New Orleans, where they would face the New England Patriots. Favre battled the flu in the week leading up

**VERY SPECIAL** Return specialist Desmond Howard (81) became the first special teams player to win Super Bowl MVP.

to the game. But come game time, he was well enough to throw for 246 yards and two touchdowns. It was Howard, however, the special-teamer extraordinaire, who was the game's MVP. He racked up a Super Bowl–record 244 return yards, including a record 99-yard kickoff return for a score at the end of the third quarter. The touchdown secured the Pack's 35–21 victory.

"This is a team that plays together, and for that reason we deserve this," said Packers tight end Keith Jackson. "Nobody is more important than anybody else, whether you're Reggie White or Brett Favre or a guy blocking on special teams. We don't get down on anyone else for making mistakes, and for that reason people don't worry about messing up. That's rare. I wish every junior high school and high school team could be around this and sniff this and sense what it's like to be a champion."

# #10

## 1950 *Cleveland*
# BROWNS

**COACH**
Paul Brown

**RECORD**
10–2

**1950 NFL CHAMPIONS**

When the Browns joined the NFL in 1950, they were coming off four championships in the All-America Football Conference. Cleveland was one of three AAFC teams joining the NFL that season. While the AAFC wasn't considered as strong a league as the NFL, the Browns quickly showed that they not only belonged but were also flat-out better than everyone. "[They] are the greatest football club I ever saw," NFL commissioner Bert Bell said upon witnessing Cleveland beat the defending NFL champion Philadelphia Eagles 35–10 in the opener of the 1950 season.

Cleveland's coach, Paul Brown, had a more measured response. "We are not going to gloat," he said. "This is only the start of a season. We have plenty of games left to play."

Despite that humble attitude, the Browns were the team to beat. Three games into the 1950 season, someone *did* beat them, however. The New York Giants defeated the Browns 6–0 in Cleveland. New York scored a touchdown in the first quarter and then, as one newspaper story put it, "held on for dear life."

The Giants, as it turned out, were

**IT'S GOOD**
Kicker Lou Groza booted the winning
field goal in the 1950 NFL Championship
Game with 28 seconds left.

## PLAYBOOK INSIDER

On a snowy December day at Cleveland Municipal Stadium, with the score tied 3–3 in the Browns' American Conference playoff game against the Giants, New York prepared for Cleveland QB **Otto Graham** to try to win the game through the air. Instead, he rushed for 37 yards in three attempts to put kicker Lou Groza in position to help win the game in the final minute.

## UNSUNG HERO

Cleveland guard **Bill Willis** was one of the first four African-Americans to play pro football since the 1930s, along with teammate Marion Motley. In the Browns' playoff game against the Giants, Willis made a key tackle at the Cleveland four-yard line to save a touchdown. Willis was later inducted into the Hall of Fame.

## HUT, HUT, WHAT??

The ground was so icy in the Browns-Giants' playoff game that players from both teams wore basketball shoes to try to gain extra traction. Browns kicker **Lou Groza** had two different shoes: He wore a football shoe without cleats on his kicking foot and one with cleats on his plant foot.

the only team that could beat these Browns. They met again in Week 6—Cleveland won two games in the interim—and again New York prevailed, this time at the Polo Grounds in Harlem, 17–13. "The better team won," Brown said.

But Brown, as one Ohio sportswriter put it, was "allergic to losing." Cleveland went on a six-game winning streak to finish the regular season 10–2.

Fullback Marion Motley, who had led the Browns in rushing since the team was founded, in 1946, ran for an NFL-best 810 yards. Halfback Dub Jones led the team with 11 touchdowns (six rushing, five receiving). And Otto Graham threw 14 TDs, scoring another six times with his feet.

### GIANT REMATCH

Guess who else finished the season 10–2? Yup. The Giants! The two would have to meet (again) to decide who would represent the American Conference in the NFL title game. Despite Cleveland's two losses to New York, the Browns were favored by seven points going into the matchup, which would take place in Cleveland.

## IN THE CLEVELAND BROWNS, WE PROBABLY HAVE THE MOST INTENSELY COACHED CLUB IN HISTORY."

—NFL COMMISSIONER **BERT BELL**, FOLLOWING THE 1950 CHAMPIONSHIP GAME

The third time was indeed the charm. Kicker Lou Groza hit two field goals, the second with 58 seconds remaining, and the Browns sealed an 8–6 victory on a safety with eight seconds left.

The NFL Championship Game, on the other hand, was an offensive showcase. The Browns and the Los Angeles Rams went down to the wire. Rams quarterback Bob Waterfield threw for 312 yards and a touchdown. Graham countered with

298 passing yards and four scores despite a 28-mph wind whipping through Cleveland Municipal Stadium on December 24.

With his team down 28–27 and just under three minutes to play, Graham fumbled on the Rams' 17-yard line. Graham thought he had ruined his team's chances. "I wanted to crawl into a hole," he said afterward. "I wouldn't have given anything for our chances at that time." But Christmas came early for the Browns. They would get the ball back, and with 28 seconds remaining, Groza hit a 16-yard field goal to win it all.

Cleveland prevailed 30–28. "This was an instance when a magnificently coached club, which just wouldn't give up, overcame great opposition," Commissioner Bell said. "The Browns were ready for anything. I'd say they have that extra something that makes champions."

It was the start of a special era in Cleveland. The Browns were champions again in 1954 and 1955 and were back in the NFL title game in six of the next seven seasons.

**READY TO ROLL**
Coming off a loss in
Super Bowl V, the
Cowboys entered the
1971 season determined
to win the championship.

# #11

## 1971 *Dallas* COWBOYS

There's an old saying in football: "If you have two quarterbacks, you have no quarterbacks." This was the situation the Dallas Cowboys found themselves in heading into the 1971 season. There was Craig Morton, a 28-year-old drop-back passer who had started the majority of games over the past two seasons and led Dallas to Super Bowl V, where the team lost to the Baltimore Colts.

Then there was 29-year-old Roger Staubach, the 1963 Heisman Trophy winner, who had started four games

**COACH**
Tom Landry

**RECORD**
11–3

**SUPER BOWL VI CHAMPIONS**

total. Staubach, who could make plays with his arm and his feet, was entering only his third NFL season. After graduating from the Naval Academy, he had served during the Vietnam War and did not join the Cowboys full-time until 1969.

Dallas coach Tom Landry couldn't make up his mind and said the team would have two Number 1 quarterbacks. Morton started the first game—and won. Staubach got the start the following week, but he was hit so hard on his first pass attempt that he had to leave the game. Morton won that one

too. Morton started the next week, but Landry replaced him in the third quarter of a losing effort. The week after, Staubach started, but Landry pulled him in the second half.

Back and forth they went, until finally the members of the Dallas defense chose linebacker Lee Roy Jordan to speak to Landry about the situation. After stumbling through three losses in five weeks, the players wanted a quarterback—one quarterback—to lead the team.

Before the Cowboys' Week 8 matchup against the St. Louis Cardinals, Landry chose a starter: Staubach. Dallas won the next seven games.

## LEADER OF THE HERD

In 1971, defensive tackle **Bob Lilly** played his seventh All-Pro season. He never missed a game in his 14-year career, which was played entirely with the Cowboys. In 1980 he became the first Cowboys player inducted into the Hall of Fame.

## STATS INCREDIBLE!

# 20.3

Average points by which Dallas defeated its opponents over the final six games of the 1971 regular season.

## HUT, HUT, WHAT??

The Cowboys played their first game in **Texas Stadium** in 1971. The stadium, which would be the team's home until 2008, had a large hole in the roof so that the fans were covered but the players were not.

## BREAKING THROUGH

The Cowboys made the postseason every season from 1966 through 1970.

"But what do we have to show for it?" asked Dan Reeves, the team's player-coach. "Zip!"

Yes, five years in a row, the Cowboys had fallen short of a title—including once in the Super Bowl and twice in the NFL Championship Game. (Before the AFL and the NFL merged in 1970, each league had its own championship game and the winners of those games would meet in what would become known as the Super Bowl.)

Dallas wasn't interested in being a runner-up anymore. In the 1971 playoffs, the Cowboys were businesslike in their 20–12 defeat of the Minnesota Vikings, then defeated the San Francisco 49ers 14–3. Next up: the Super Bowl against the Miami Dolphins.

"The Dolphins are a well-coached young football team," Reeves said before the game. "That makes it fairly easy to prepare for them. Because they are disciplined and well-coached, you know exactly what they are going to do."

After studying Miami's defensive habits in their film sessions, the

"

# WE WERE 4–3, AND ALL OF A SUDDEN WE WERE SUPER BOWL CHAMPIONS."

—DALLAS QUARTERBACK
ROGER STAUBACH, DESCRIBING
THE TEAM'S TURNAROUND

Cowboys piled up 252 yards on the ground, behind running backs Duane Thomas (95 yards) and Walt Garrison (74). Staubach completed 12 of 19 passes for 119 yards and two touchdowns, earning game MVP honors.

On defense, Dallas relied on 11-year veteran tackle Bob Lilly,

Jordan, and linebacker Chuck Howley, who was the Super Bowl MVP the year before. (Howley is still the only player from a losing team to receive the award.) The Cowboys stopped Miami from getting anything going and held the Dolphins to a single field goal. Dallas remains the only team in the Super Bowl's 52-year history to not let its opponent reach the end zone.

After the game was over, Dallas players hoisted Landry onto their shoulders. The Cowboys had found their quarterback and were victors at last.

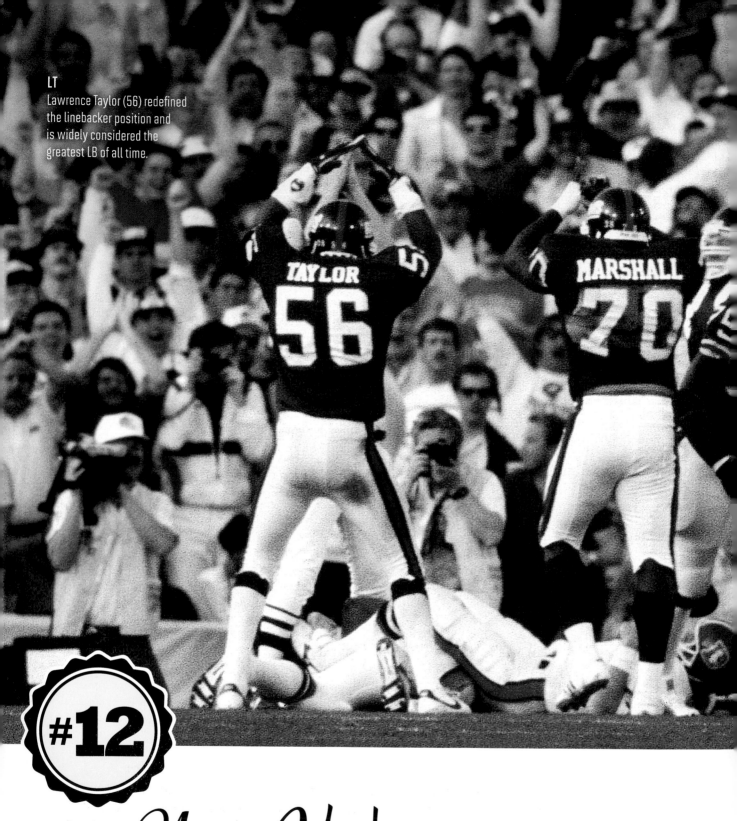

# #12

# 1986 *New York*
# GIANTS

COACH
Bill
Parcells

RECORD
14–2

SUPER BOWL XXI
CHAMPIONS

In 1986, the New York Giants were a team defined mostly by its defense. And that defense, guided by coordinator and future New England Patriots head coach Bill Belichick, was defined by its linebackers.

While most great linebacking groups were made up of just three players, the Giants rotated eight LBs. The linebackers were anchored by future Hall of Famers Lawrence Taylor and Harry Carson, as well as Carl Banks and Pepper Johnson. Taylor revolutionized the position. In 1986, he became the first defensive player to be named consensus NFL MVP. "Who else is there?" Don Shula, the coach of the Miami Dolphins, once asked. "Taylor could be the best ever."

The Giants made it nearly impossible for opposing offenses to move the chains. In the divisional round of the playoffs against Joe Montana and the San Francisco 49ers, the Giants allowed just two of 14 third-down conversions.

**ON TARGET**
Giants quarterback Phil Simms (11) completed a Super Bowl–record 22 of 25 passes against the Broncos.

## UNSUNG HERO

**Phil McConkey** had been a special teams ace but never a star receiver. That changed in the Super Bowl. In the second half, he caught a 44-yard flea-flicker that set up the Giants' third touchdown. On New York's next drive, McConkey scored a six-yard TD, putting the game away for good.

## PLAYBOOK INSIDER

One of the biggest plays of the Giants' 1986 season didn't happen on offense or defense. It was on special teams. In a preview of the Super Bowl matchup against the Denver Broncos in Week 12, no offensive touchdowns were scored. It was kicker **Raul Allegre's 34-yard field goal** in the fourth quarter that gave the Giants a 19–16 win—and the confidence to know they could do it again.

## HUT, HUT, WHAT??

Next time you see excited players dumping Gatorade on their coach, think of the 1986 Giants. They were the first team to do it regularly. Team captain **Harry Carson** initiated the tradition, which took place after every one of the Giants' 17 regular-season and playoff wins.

> ## LAWRENCE TAYLOR, SO STRONG, SO INVINCIBLE. HE COULD DO ANYTHING. HE'D SOAR 10 FEET IN THE AIR TO BLOCK PUNTS, LEAP OVER PILES, TACKLE THREE PEOPLE AT ONCE."
>
> —STEVE STREATER, TAYLOR'S TEAMMATE AT THE UNIVERSITY OF NORTH CAROLINA

Against the Washington Redskins in the conference championship, the Giants didn't allow a single third- or fourth-down conversion in 18 tries.

## JEERS TO CHEERS

When the Giants met the Denver Broncos in Super Bowl XXI, New York's defense came up huge again. The Giants sacked Denver quarterback John Elway three times and intercepted him once. But it was New York's own QB, Phil Simms, who clinched the game. Before the Super Bowl, Phil Simms was considered a good, but not great, quarterback. Injuries limited his play, and Giants fans even booed him.

After Simms's unimpressive performances in the first two playoff games, those fans probably thought they would need New York's defense to carry the team again. But when it mattered most, in the Super Bowl, Simms lived up to his potential.

Simms had one of the greatest games ever by a quarterback. He completed 22 of 25 passes, a Super Bowl record, for 268 yards and three touchdowns. Simms's completion percentage would have been even higher if one of his receivers hadn't tripped.

"He quarterbacked as good a game as ever has been played," said Bill Parcells, the Giants' head coach. Said Giants center Bart Oates, "Phil had this strange sort of glow. It was like he was in a perfect biorhythm stage or something." It was an easy call to name Simms the Super Bowl MVP.

Of course, the Giants' defense was great too. Defensive tackle George Martin sacked Elway in the end zone for a safety in the second quarter. The Broncos scored only two touchdowns, and the second came with two minutes left, when the game was already in hand. The Giants won the game by a final score of 39–20.

The legacy of the 1986 team lives on through its players, and also through its coaches. Parcells's assistant coaches on the team included not only Belichick but also former Cleveland Browns head coach Romeo Crennel.

**TD FOR TD**
Terrell Davis (30) led the NFL in rushing touchdowns in 1998 and ran for at least 100 yards in 11 games.

# #13

**1998** *Denver*

# BRONCOS

When you win the Super Bowl, what do you do for an encore the following season? Win another one, of course. That's exactly what the Denver Broncos did in 1998. They improved upon their 12–4 record from a season earlier and allowed future Hall of Fame quarterback John Elway to retire as a back-to-back champ.

In 1998, Denver just kept winning... and winning... and winning. The Broncos were especially tough on the ground. After rushing for 75 yards in the season opener, running back Terrell Davis had seven straight games with at least 100 yards. He finished the season with 11 100-yard games.

Even when hamstring, rib, and back injuries forced the 38-year-old Elway to miss four starts in the middle of the season, backup Bubby Brister stepped in and won all four games. Both Denver QBs had the benefit of throwing to receivers Rod Smith (1,222 yards) and Ed McCaffrey (1,053), who each had the best season of their careers up until that point.

In Week 14, Denver beat the Kansas City Chiefs 35–31 after Elway led two scoring drives in the final seven minutes. The Broncos improved to 13–0, earned home field advantage throughout the playoffs, and secured a first-round bye.

Only the 1934 Chicago Bears and the 1972 Dolphins had ever made it to 13–0.

One week later, the Broncos lost to the New York Giants, but the Denver players didn't mope around afterward. "Give me 18–1, that's what I want," said tight end Shannon Sharpe. "Because they don't give out rings or Lombardi Trophies to people who go 16–0 in the regular season."

The Broncos lost again the following week, to the Miami Dolphins. The Wednesday after the game, Elway had a talk with the offense.

**COACH**
Mike Shanahan

**RECORD**
14–2

**SUPER BOWL XXXIII CHAMPIONS**

## HUT, HUT, WHAT??

Running back **Terrell Davis** had a signature touchdown celebration: Whenever Davis made it to the end zone, he saluted his teammates. The Mile High Salute gained national attention when the Broncos won their back-to-back Super Bowls in the late 1990s.

## PLAYBOOK INSIDER

Having lost to the Dolphins four weeks earlier, Denver wasn't about to fall to Miami again in the first round of the playoffs. The Broncos quickly put the game out of reach with their dominant ground attack. Denver scored **three rushing touchdowns** on its first three possessions. The score was 21–3 at halftime and ended up 38–3.

## UNSUNG HERO

In 1998, Denver's Pro Bowl kicker, **Jason Elam**, made more extra points (58) than he did in any other season over his 17-year career. With the Broncos winning games by an average of two touchdowns or more, Elam's field goal skills weren't often needed. But in a 37–24 win over the Jacksonville Jaguars in Week 8, Elam showed how powerful his kicking leg was. Elam booted a 63-yarder through the uprights, tying the NFL record for the longest in league history.

"Somebody had blown the fire out," Smith said. "John said we didn't have enough fire under us. Somebody relit it, and it might have been when John told us to just go back out and have fun. That kind of took the pressure off of us."

Denver closed out the regular season with a win over the Seattle Seahawks. In the game, Davis became the fourth back in NFL history to gain more than 2,000 yards in a season (2,008). He also led the league with 21 rushing touchdowns. Elway's four TD passes in the season finale earned him membership in the "300 club" for passing touchdowns, which at the time had only two other members.

## FANNING THE FLAMES

Somebody had certainly relit the fire under the Broncos. They defeated Miami in the divisional round (Davis rushed for 199 yards), then beat the New York Jets (Davis went for 167). Elway threw for 355 yards and two touchdowns over the two games, but it was Davis, that season's NFL MVP, who caught the eye of the Atlanta Falcons' coaching staff leading up

> "EVERYWHERE I WENT, PEOPLE WOULD ASK, 'YOU GUYS GOING UNDEFEATED?' AND I ALWAYS TOLD THEM, 'I DON'T KNOW. I JUST WANT TO WIN THE SUPER BOWL.'"
>
> —BRONCOS DEFENSIVE TACKLE **KEITH TRAYLOR**

to Super Bowl XXXIII.

Never mind that Elway was about to become the first quarterback to start five Super Bowls. (He lost the first three.) "All week long, all the Falcons talked about was stopping our running game," Elway said after the Broncos beat the Falcons 34–19. "I knew they were saying, 'Make Elway beat us.' My thought was, Good, let's go. I was so motivated, it wasn't even funny."

Elway went out and threw for 336 yards and a touchdown to cap off his 16-year NFL career with a Super Bowl MVP award. Davis, who had been MVP of the previous year's big game, rushed for 102 yards.

From the balcony of his hotel room several hours later, Elway reflected on the evening. "I never thought it could get any better than last year, but just look at this scene," he said, pointing to fans celebrating in front of the team's hotel. "You couldn't have planned it more perfectly—no wind during the game, warm weather, a full moon—and now it pours, like a great, big release. I never, ever thought I would be the Super Bowl MVP."

**OUT ON TOP**
Quarterback John Elway (7) retired after leading Denver to back-to-back championships.

# #14

## 1999 *St. Louis*

# RAMS

L osing your starting quarterback before the season even starts is never a good sign. It's even worse when you replace him with an unproven playcaller who had been working in a grocery store just five years earlier. But none of that mattered to the St. Louis Rams and Kurt Warner.

After being cut by the Green Bay Packers, Warner bounced around the Arena Football League and NFL Europe before becoming a backup QB for the Rams. When starter Trent Green injured his knee in the 1999 preseason, Warner stepped in and didn't let the opportunity go to waste. In his first game, he

**COACH**
Dick
Vermeil

**RECORD**
13–3

**SUPER BOWL XXXIV
CHAMPIONS**

**DO IT ALL**
St. Louis's Marshall Faulk
(28) became the second
player in NFL history
with at least 1,000 yards
rushing and receiving.

threw for 309 yards in a win against Baltimore. In his fourth game, he threw for five touchdowns in a win over the 49ers. Warner's rags-to-riches story quickly made him a household name as he led one of the most productive offenses of all time.

Costarring with Warner in the Greatest Show on Turf were future Hall of Fame running back Marshall Faulk (1,381 rushing yards, 1,048 receiving yards) and a

# IT'S BEEN THE CHARACTER OF THIS TEAM ALL YEAR. THE BIG PLAY. TODAY IT WON A SUPER BOWL FOR US."

—**ERNIE CONWELL**, RAMS TIGHT END, DESCRIBING THE TEAM'S HIGHLIGHT-WORTHY SEASON

devastating receiving duo in Isaac Bruce (1,165 yards) and Torry Holt (788). In 1999, the Rams' 526 points were nearly double their total from the previous season. They became one of only four teams in NFL history to score more than 30 points 12 times in a season, and Warner became the second quarterback to throw for at least 40 touchdowns in a season (41).

The final play of Super Bowl XXXIV is now known simply as The Tackle. With time running out, Titans quarterback Steve McNair completed a pass to his second option, Kevin Dyson, on the right side of the field. St. Louis linebacker Mike Jones read the play perfectly and **made a diving tackle** to pull Dyson down by his waist at the one-yard line.

### STATS INCREDIBLE!

**526** Points scored by the Rams in 1999, the second-most all time. Since St. Louis played home games in a dome, its high-powered offense earned the nickname the Greatest Show on Turf.

### LEADER OF THE HERD

Even though he had only attempted 11 passes total before becoming the Rams' starting QB, **Kurt Warner** went on to become league MVP. He threw 41 touchdowns, becoming only the second quarterback to throw at least 40.

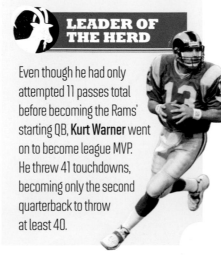

## A GAME OF INCHES

When St. Louis advanced to Super Bowl XXXIV against the Tennessee Titans, it was tough to know which Rams team would show up. St. Louis had lost the final game of the regular season, then bounced back to score 49 points in the divisional playoffs. That was followed by just 11 in the conference championship game.

Super Bowl XXXIV would go down as one of the most exciting title games ever. While the Rams' offense received most of the attention, their defense was also a force. St. Louis returned seven interceptions for touchdowns, the third-most in league history. And when the Super Bowl was on the line at the end of the game, the Rams' D came up huge.

With just six seconds left and the Rams up 23–16, the Titans drove the ball to St. Louis's six-yard line. A touchdown would win the game.

Titans quarterback Steve McNair found receiver Kevin Dyson. He had just one man to beat. But St. Louis linebacker Mike Jones wrapped up a lunging Dyson at the one-yard line as time ran out. "It seemed like slow motion," Jones said after the game. "I couldn't see McNair throw the ball, but I could feel it."

It was a fairy-tale finish for a team that only one year earlier had finished 4–12. Despite his unlikely path to becoming a Super Bowl champion, Warner never stopped believing in himself or his team.

"How can you be in awe of something that you expect yourself to do?" Warner said after the Super Bowl. "People think this season is the first time I touched a football; they don't realize I've been doing this for years."

# #15

**1940** *Chicago*

# BEARS

**T FOR TOUCHDOWN**
The Bears (in white) used
a T formation on offense
to confuse opponents.

**COACH**
George
Halas

--------

**RECORD**
8–3

--------

**1940 NFL
CHAMPIONS**

n football, not many offensive schemes become immortalized in song. But the Chicago Bears' offense in 1940 was so thrilling that it inspired Al Hoffman to include the lyrics, "We'll never forget the way you thrilled the nation, with your T formation" in the team's fight song, "Bear Down, Chicago Bears."

The T formation was popular in college football in the 1930s and led to some impressive offensive outputs. Bears coach

George Halas helped develop it for the NFL game, and the results in 1940 were even more astounding. Chicago lined up three running backs behind quarterback Sid Luckman, who was behind the center. Any of the three backs could receive the ball, which opened up a lot of different possibilities. Luckman said that the Bears' playbook gave him more than 1,000 options for plays. You can imagine how hard it was for opposing defenses

## LEADER OF THE HERD

Chicago's six-foot quarterback **Sid Luckman** was part of an offensive revolution. In 1940, he threw for 941 yards, an impressive stat at a time when NFL teams focused primarily on rushing. With Luckman running the T formation in the championship game, the Bears' offense had 519 total yards.

## STATS INCREDIBLE!

# 73

**Points scored** by the Bears in their shutout of the Washington Redskins in the 1940 NFL Championship Game. In the Super Bowl era, the highest *combined* point total is 75. The San Francisco 49ers defeated the San Diego Chargers 49–26 in Super Bowl XXIX.

## HUT, HUT, WHAT??

**Dick Plasman** was a tight end on the 1940 Bears who caught 11 passes for 245 yards and two touchdowns. But Plasman is more famous for being the last person to play in the NFL without a helmet. The NFL made a rule requiring players to wear helmets in 1943.

**73–0**
The Bears and coach George Halas (in suit) had reason to celebrate after winning 73–0 in the NFL championship.

to figure out which one Chicago was actually going to run.

Nowhere was this more apparent than in the NFL Championship Game.

## TOTAL DOMINATION

The 1940 NFL title game was a rematch of a regular-season matchup between the Bears and the Washington Redskins. The two teams had met three weeks earlier at Washington's Griffith Stadium. That first game was a defensive showdown that Washington won 7–3. It was the only time all season that the Bears hadn't scored a touchdown.

The loss must have lit a fire under the Chicago offense. In the final two games of the regular season, the Bears scored 47 and 31 points, respectively. But the team was just getting started.

In the rematch against Washington for the championship, Chicago began its domination early. Bill Osmanski ran 68 yards for a touchdown on the second play of the game. The Bears added two more touchdowns in the first quarter. Luckman scored from the one-yard line, and back Joe Maniaci ran 42 yards for another touchdown. By halftime, Chicago had increased its lead to 28–0.

The Bears kept up the attack. Even though Coach Halas took the starters out, the Bears still scored 45 points in the second half. That included three interception returns for TDs and two touchdown rushes of 23 yards or more. It was such an offensive explosion that officials stopped allowing the Bears to kick extra points because too many balls had been lost in the stands following the point after attempts!

The final score was 73–0. It is still the largest margin of victory in NFL history and the most points scored by one team in any game. The Bears scored seven rushing touchdowns in the game—the second-most ever.

Chicago's defense deserves credit too. In addition to the three pick sixes, the Bears held Sammy Baugh, who led the league in passing yards, touchdowns, and completion percentage, to just 102 yards through the air.

It's unlikely that we'll ever see another 73–0 rout in a championship game. But if we do, there will probably be a novel offensive scheme like the T formation leading the way—and a song to commemorate the occasion.

# #16

## 2013 *Seattle*

# SEAHAWKS

**COACH**
Pete
Carroll

**RECORD**
13–3

**SUPER BOWL XLVIII
CHAMPIONS**

They called themselves the Legion of Boom. But based on their backgrounds, the members of the Seattle Seahawks' secondary in 2013 did not seem that intimidating. The unit was made up of misfits. Cornerback Richard Sherman was a former wide receiver who wasn't drafted until the fifth round in 2011. Opposing corner Brandon Browner played in the Canadian Football League, and safety Kam Chancellor used to play quarterback. At 5'10" fellow safety Earl Thomas was considered a bit too small to be an impact player.

None of that mattered. The Legion of Boom put on a defensive display for the ages, making opposing teams pay dearly for trying to throw against it. "We're in a league of our own," said Chancellor. The quartet combined for 17 interceptions in 2013 and helped Seattle lead the NFL in just about every defensive category. Sherman, Chancellor, and Thomas were all selected to the Pro Bowl. Of course, they didn't play in the all-star game because they had another "bowl" game they were focused on: the Super Bowl.

## LOWERING THE BOOM

The Seahawks rolled through the NFC playoffs, setting up a Super Bowl XLVIII showdown with Peyton Manning and the Denver Broncos. The Broncos were an offensive juggernaut. They were coming off a season in which they scored 606 points, the most in NFL history. Denver averaged 457.3 yards per game, second-best all time. And Manning set a single-season NFL record with 55 touchdown passes and won his fifth MVP award.

It took all of 12 seconds for the Seahawks' defense to show they were up to the challenge. Facing the fierce Seattle D-line, Denver center Manny Ramirez snapped the ball over Manning's head on the first play from scrimmage. Denver running back Knowshon Moreno recovered the ball and was tackled in the end zone for a safety. It was the fastest score in Super Bowl history. The Seahawks never looked back.

By halftime, Manning had thrown two interceptions, including a 69-yard pick six to linebacker Malcolm Smith. The Seahawks were on their way to the most lopsided win in a Super Bowl in nearly 30 years.

On offense, Seattle was led by quarterback Russell Wilson, who was as dangerous with his legs as he was with his throwing arm. He tossed 26 touchdown passes and rushed for 539 yards during the season. In the Super Bowl, the second-year QB threw for 206 yards and two touchdowns, hitting eight different receivers.

Running back Marshawn Lynch used his Beast Mode style of play to anchor the ground game for Seattle.

The Seahawks were great even on special teams. Percy Harvin started the second half of the Super Bowl with an 87-yard kickoff return for a score.

But as it had all season long, Seattle's defense stole the show in the championship game. When Seahawks linebacker K.J. Wright studied film of the Broncos for the first time, he thought, *Man, we already got this game won.* Three players on the Seattle defense each had at least 10 tackles in the Super Bowl. So it was fitting that when Smith became the 10th defensive player to win Super Bowl MVP, he refused to look at it as a personal honor. Smith—who had 10 tackles and the crucial interception—did play great. But according to him, he was simply "representing the defense." It's a defense that will go down as one of the greatest of all time.

> ## EVERYONE ON THIS TEAM HAS A CHIP ON HIS SHOULDER. THAT'S WHAT MAKES THIS TEAM: GUYS ARE HUNGRY. GUYS HAVE ASPIRATIONS TO BE GREAT."
>
> —WALTER THURMOND, SEATTLE CORNERBACK

### UNSUNG HERO

Receiver **Doug Baldwin** was undrafted out of college. But in 2013, he was the heart of the Seattle receiving corps. Baldwin was second on the team with 778 receiving yards and tied for the team lead with five receiving touchdowns. He added 202 yards and a score in the playoffs.

### STATS INCREDIBLE!

**12** **Seconds it took** for the Seahawks to score in Super Bowl XLVIII, the fastest score in Super Bowl history. On the game's first play from scrimmage, Seattle tackled Broncos running back Knowshon Moreno in the end zone for a safety.

### LEADER OF THE HERD

Some felt **Russell Wilson**, at only 5'11", was too short to play quarterback in the NFL. Wilson silenced critics during Seattle's playoff run, when he threw three TDs and zero interceptions.

# #17

## 1976 *Oakland*
# RAIDERS

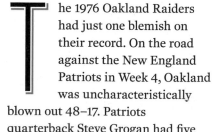

**COACH**
John
Madden

**RECORD**
13–1

**SUPER BOWL XI
CHAMPIONS**

The 1976 Oakland Raiders had just one blemish on their record. On the road against the New England Patriots in Week 4, Oakland was uncharacteristically blown out 48–17. Patriots quarterback Steve Grogan had five touchdowns (two rushing, three passing), and running back Sam Cunningham gained 101 yards on the ground. It was the only time all season that the Raiders allowed more than 28 points in a game. Afterward, Oakland coach John Madden was in a state of awe. "It's like playing against a seven-man line all day," he said of the Patriots. "Devastating."

The Raiders never came close to losing a game again that season. They reeled off 10 straight wins to

**GROUND RAID**
Oakland running back
Mark van Eeghen (30)
hit his stride late in the
1976 season.

## STATS INCREDIBLE!

**8** Future Hall of Famers on the 1976 Raiders roster: Fred Biletnikoff, Willie Brown, Dave Casper, Ray Guy, Ted Hendricks, Art Shell, Ken Stabler, and Gene Upshaw. Coach John Madden and owner Al Davis were also inducted.

## LEADER OF THE HERD

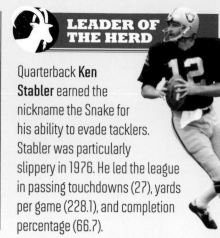

Quarterback **Ken Stabler** earned the nickname the Snake for his ability to evade tacklers. Stabler was particularly slippery in 1976. He led the league in passing touchdowns (27), yards per game (228.1), and completion percentage (66.7).

## UNSUNG HERO

**Fred Biletnikoff's** stats were not as impressive as those of his fellow receivers Dave Casper and Cliff Branch in 1976. But Biletnikoff came up big in the Super Bowl. Against the Vikings, the 33-year-old receiver led the team with 79 receiving yards, 48 of which came on a single catch.

close out the regular season. Oakland was firing on all cylinders. In the Raiders' final three games before the playoffs, they won by 33-, 15-, and 24-point margins.

So perhaps it was fitting that the Raiders' first-round opponent in the 1976 playoffs would be—you guessed it—the Patriots.

### SILVER-AND-BLACK ATTACK

The 1976 Raiders were once voted the greatest team of all time by NFL.com. But they still had their issues with the Patriots. In the third quarter of the divisional playoff game, the Pats held a 21–10 lead. This was despite the fact that the game was played in Oakland, where the Raiders had won more than 85% of their regular-season games and seven of nine playoff games over the previous 10 seasons.

But great teams don't always cruise through a game or season. Sometimes, their greatness is revealed through the challenges they overcome. Raiders running back Mark van Eeghen, who grew up in New England, scored a touchdown in the fourth quarter to bring the game to within a score.

## WE KNEW IT HAD TO BE WON IN THE PIT. WE KNEW IF WE COULD RUN AT 'EM, SNAKE WOULD GET 'EM ON THE PASSING."

—OAKLAND GUARD **GENE UPSHAW**, AFTER SUPER BOWL XI

Van Eeghen rushed for 1,012 yards that season but played particularly well down the stretch. "In our last six or seven games, he's finally learned to lose some of his tightness," said Madden.

It fell to Oakland quarterback Ken Stabler, the NFL Player of the Year in 1976, to secure the victory. Nicknamed the Snake for his ability to slither past defenders, Stabler scrambled into the end zone from the one-yard line to give the Raiders a 24–21 victory.

With the Patriots vanquished, Oakland returned to its dominating ways, rolling past the Pittsburgh Steelers 24–7 in the conference championship and the Minnesota Vikings 32–14 in Super Bowl XI.

Oakland's victory in the Super Bowl led to one of the most famous photographs in football history. Cameras captured Coach Madden being carried off the field by his players, his arm waving in the air. Madden, of course, would go on to become a popular broadcaster and the face of the popular video game series. His team, stocked with future Hall of Famers, would go on to be remembered as one of the best ever.

**THE PATRIOT WAY**
Tom Brady (12) and the Patriots overcame adversity all season to become Super Bowl champs.

#18

2016 New England

# PATRIOTS

COACH
Bill
Belichick

RECORD
14–2

SUPER BOWL LI
CHAMPIONS

The word "miracle" gets tossed around a lot in sports, but for the 2016 New England Patriots, it's appropriate.

Before 2016, the Patriots had lost the conference championship game in three of the past four seasons. The team's struggles continued in 2016. New England's franchise player, quarterback Tom Brady, missed the first four games of the season due to a suspension. The team was also without defensive stars Chandler Jones and Jamie Collins, who were traded away. Starting left tackle Sebastian Vollmer missed the season with a hip injury, and superstar tight end Rob Gronkowski missed the entire playoffs with a back injury.

So when New England was down 25 points to the Atlanta Falcons with 8:31 left in the third quarter of Super Bowl LI, it seemed as if it would take a miracle to win.

The Falcons had scored the seventh-most points in NFL history during the season. New England's chances of winning the game were a minuscule 0.3%.

But the Patriots believed in miracles, and themselves. Two touchdowns, one two-point conversion, and one field goal helped New England close the gap to 28–20.

That's when Pats receiver Julian Edelman reeled in a truly miraculous catch. Teammate Martellus Bennett said Edelman caught the ball "between seven guys' legs." The pass was initially deflected by a Falcons defender, causing Edelman to adjust his route and dive over three defenders to catch the ball just before it touched the ground. That led to the tying touchdown with less than a minute left in regulation.

By the time the first overtime in Super Bowl history started, there was no way the Patriots were going to be denied. James White scored a two-yard touchdown just four minutes into the extra period, and the Pats won 34–28. "Just an avalanche," Brady said of his team's incredible comeback.

## COMEBACK KIDS

During the regular season, Brady became the NFL's all-time leader in wins by a quarterback (201). He also set seven Super Bowl records, including passing yards (486) and total touchdown passes (15). The Patriots established themselves as not only the best team of the 21st century but also perhaps the most dominant dynasty of all time. Since 2001, the Pats have won five Super Bowls. Only the Steelers have more Super Bowl victories—and they won their first in 1974.

The 2016 Patriots will be remembered for more than just finishing 14–2 with the top-rated defense and third-ranked offense. What allowed the team to pull off such an improbable win is that everyone contributed. Yes, they had one of the greatest quarterbacks and head coaches of all time in Brady and Bill Belichick. But New England also relied on a key sack from unheralded defensive end Trey Flowers and an out-of-nowhere performance from running back James White.

At halftime of Super Bowl LI, with the Patriots trailing 21–3, safety Duron Harmon reportedly said that New England would pull off the "greatest comeback of all time."

Harmon was right. The Patriots battled back, and by accomplishing the greatest comeback of all time, they established themselves as one of the greatest teams of all time.

> ## "THIS ONE WAS DEFINITELY THE SWEETEST."
>
> —**ROBERT KRAFT**, PATRIOTS OWNER, ABOUT NEW ENGLAND'S FIFTH SUPER BOWL VICTORY

---

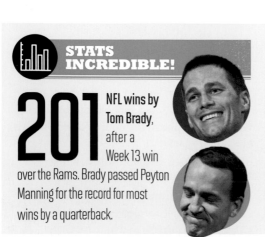

### 📊 STATS INCREDIBLE!

# 201

NFL wins by Tom Brady, after a Week 13 win over the Rams. Brady passed Peyton Manning for the record for most wins by a quarterback.

### 🏈 HUT, HUT, WHAT??

Tom Brady couldn't find **an important souvenir** from Super Bowl LI. After the game, the jersey he wore during the game was stolen from the Patriots' locker room. Investigators eventually found the thief, and Brady had his jersey returned two months after the game.

### 🏃 UNSUNG HERO

**James White** had five touchdowns all season long heading into Super Bowl LI. In the big game, the running back scored three times, including the game-winner in overtime. He also set a Super Bowl record for catches by a running back (14).

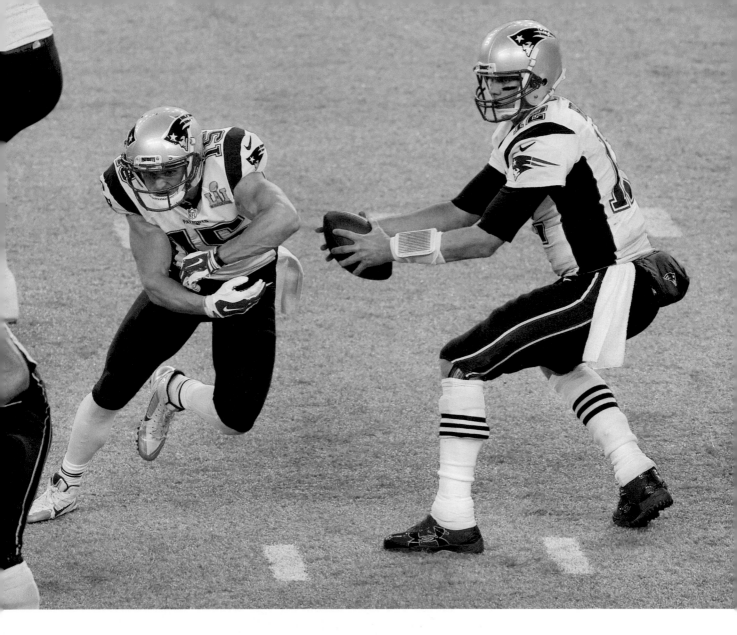

## TOM TERRIFIC
Trailing by 25 points, Brady (above, with ball) led an incredible Super Bowl comeback with help from Julian Edelman's miraculous catch (left).

# #19

## 2000 Baltimore RAVENS

**COACH**
Brian Billick

**RECORD**
12-4

**SUPER BOWL XXXV CHAMPIONS**

Defense wins championships, the saying goes. But good luck winning anything without a quarterback.

The 2000 Ravens had a great defense when the season started. Led by two future Hall of Famers, linebacker Ray Lewis and safety Rod Woodson, Baltimore's starting 11 had the potential to be among the best ever. The offense had the potential to be a disaster.

Five of the Ravens' first seven games were on the road. The Ravens went 5–2 in that span, posting three shutouts. Quickly, however, the team realized that its passing attack was a problem. For the entire month of October—a stretch of five complete games—the Ravens did not score a single touchdown. As they faced increasingly tougher competition, Baltimore's defense was unable to bail out its offense. Pretty soon the team was 5–4. It barely looked like a team that could make the playoffs, let alone be remembered as one of the greatest of all time.

Ravens head coach Brian Billick needed a dramatic change. So he benched starting quarterback Tony Banks for backup Trent Dilfer. The sixth overall pick in the 1994 draft, Dilfer had been a starter for the Tampa Bay Buccaneers. But he hadn't lived up to the expectations of a Top 10 draft pick.

In Week 10 against the Cincinnati Bengals, however, Dilfer gave the Ravens exactly what they needed: a touchdown. The quarterback found receiver Brandon Stokley early in the second quarter, snapping Baltimore's TD drought. He went on to throw two more touchdowns in the 27–7 win. A huge weight had been lifted off the players. Now they could go to work.

The Ravens won seven straight games to finish the regular season 12–4. The offense, led by Dilfer and his two favorite weapons, tight end Shannon Sharpe and rookie running back Jamal Lewis, provided enough scoring for the Ravens' historically stingy defense to pull out every game.

## NOWHERE TO RUN

Baltimore allowed only five rushing and 11 passing touchdowns in 2000. They conceded just 165 points, the fewest in the history of the NFL's 16-game schedule. The Ravens gave up

> # WHEN YOU GO INTO THE LION'S DEN, YOU DON'T TIPPY-TOE IN. YOU CARRY A SPEAR. YOU GO IN SCREAMING LIKE A BANSHEE."
>
> —BALTIMORE HEAD COACH **BRIAN BILLICK**

just 970 rushing yards, another NFL record. Ray Lewis's relentless pursuit of the ball helped them stifle rushing attacks all season—as did two massive players in the middle of the defensive line: Sam Adams and Tony Siragusa.

That dominance carried over into the postseason. In their wild-card game against the Denver Broncos, the Ravens allowed just 42 yards rushing on 18 attempts. Meanwhile, the offense caught some breaks, as Shannon Sharpe reeled in a deflected

**ROOKIE SENSATION**
In his first NFL season, running back Jamal Lewis (31) finished seventh in the league in rushing yards (1,364).

## PLAYBOOK INSIDER

Baltimore's game-sealing interception return for a touchdown against Tennessee in the playoffs didn't happen because a defensive back jumped a route or the opposing quarterback threw a bad pass. Eddie George was open when Titans QB Steve McNair checked down to him. With **Ray Lewis** bearing down, however, George bobbled the ball. Lewis pounced, caught the ball, and sprinted for the end zone.

## STATS INCREDIBLE!

**0**

**Players** who rushed for at least 100 yards against the Ravens all season, including in the playoffs.

## UNSUNG HERO

While the Ravens' defense deserves most of the credit for their historic season, the team wasn't going to win without offense. No single player was more responsible for Baltimore putting up points than running back **Jamal Lewis**. The fifth overall pick out of the University of Tennessee, the 21-year-old Lewis ranked seventh in the NFL with 1,364 yards as a rookie. He also had 296 yards receiving out of the backfield.

Dilfer pass and ran it half the field to the end zone. The Ravens won 21–3.

That set up a divisional round matchup against the Tennessee Titans, whom Baltimore had defeated in Week 11.

But in this game, the Ravens' offense looked like it had in October. The Titans outrushed them 126–49. In the fourth quarter, however, Baltimore's special teams and defense stepped up. A blocked field goal return and a Ray Lewis pick six gave Baltimore a 24–10 win.

In the AFC championship game against the Oakland Raiders, the defensive line punched the Ravens' ticket to the Super Bowl. Baltimore allowed just 24 rushing yards on 17 attempts, and Siragusa knocked Raiders QB Rich Gannon out of the game with a punishing hit. The Ravens' offense scored just one touchdown—a 96-yard pass from Dilfer to Sharpe—but that was all they needed.

Against the New York Giants in Super Bowl XXXV, the Ravens built an early 10–0 first-half lead with some typically solid defense and timely passing from Dilfer. Then, in the third quarter, the craziest 30 seconds in NFL history put the game away. Baltimore's Duane Starks intercepted a pass and ran it back for a 49-yard touchdown. On the ensuing kickoff, New York's Ron Dixon returned it all the way back for a score. Before you could blink, Ravens returner Jermaine Lewis had answered with a kick-return touchdown of his own.

That gave the Ravens all the momentum they needed to secure a 34–7 victory. Even more important, they had the greatest defense of all time. The Ravens' defense finished the game with four interceptions, four sacks, one touchdown scored, and no touchdowns allowed.

**#20**

**1994** *San Francisco*
# 49ERS

**COACH**
George
Seifert

------------------

**RECORD**
13–3

------------------

**SUPER BOWL XXIX
CHAMPIONS**

W hen Steve Young became San Francisco's full-time starting quarterback in the early 1990s, he did more than fill a roster spot. He replaced an icon. Young took over for Joe Montana, who had led the 49ers to four Super Bowl victories in the 1980s. Young and Montana, whom the Niners had traded to the Kansas City Chiefs in the spring of 1993, did not have the best relationship.

By 1994, Young had led the Niners to the NFC championship game twice, but that's as far as the team had gotten. In both years, San Francisco lost to the Dallas Cowboys. Young, who was known as a nice guy who didn't show a ton of emotion, faced criticism that he couldn't win big games.

In Week 2 of the 1994 season, Young and Montana met as opponents for the first time. Kansas City's D sacked Young four times, but he never quit. As Montana ran out the clock on a 24–17 win, Young was throwing up on the sideline. "He didn't have anything left," said Niners tackle Steve Wallace.

San Francisco won the next two games, and then the unthinkable happened: In Week 5, the Philadelphia Eagles pummeled the Niners. Coach George Seifert pulled Young from the game when the score was 33–8. Seifert was worried his star QB would get injured, but Young wanted a chance to fight.

Young was furious. And he told everyone on the sideline just how mad he was. This was the fiery Young fans had been looking for. "I think people were pleased to see that—that there is a human being in there," Young said later.

The effect on the team was positive. The Niners went on a tear, winning their next 10 games. That streak included a hyped rematch with San Francisco's conference title nemesis. With a 21–14 victory over the Cowboys in Week 11, San Francisco

**HIS TURN**
In 1994, 49ers QB Steve Young (8) stepped out of Joe Montana's shadow and showed he could win big games.

## LEADER OF THE HERD

The 1994 season was San Francisco quarterback **Steve Young**'s fourth in a row with a QB rating of over 100. It was also the third consecutive season that Young led the NFL in passing touchdowns (35).

## STATS INCREDIBLE!

# 131

**Points** the 49ers scored in their three games during the 1994 playoffs, an NFL record. They broke the mark set by the Niners in 1990 (126).

## HUT, HUT, WHAT??

Cornerback Deion Sanders, who signed a one-year deal with the 49ers for the 1994 season, liked to **lay his uniform out on the locker room floor** before each game. "I'm like, what is this?" recalled fellow defensive back Merton Hanks. "I had to scooch my little stool over just a little bit to make sure Deion had room to lay his socks and his pants out. Hilarious."

**SAN FRANCISCO TREAT**
Jerry Rice (80) scored three touchdowns in Super Bowl XXIX, tying his single-game record for the big game.

asserted its dominance over the NFC. "It's like you're going to school, and you've got this bully who's taking your lunch money every day," receiver Jerry Rice said after the win. "What are you going to do? Eventually you take a stand."

The 49ers played well enough to secure home field advantage and a first-round bye in the playoffs. A 44–15 beatdown of the Bears in their divisional game set up another NFC championship showdown with the Cowboys. To prepare for the big game, the 49ers needed to move their practice location to sunny Arizona after strong rains made it impossible to prepare in California.

"This organization isn't hiding its intentions," San Francisco center Bart Oates said. "We've been built with one purpose in mind: Beat Dallas."

And beat Dallas they did. The 49ers raced to a 21–0 lead and were up 31–14 at halftime. The final score of 38–28 meant Young had finally led the Niners to the big game.

## GOLD RUSH

The 49ers were huge favorites in their Super Bowl XXIX matchup against the San Diego Chargers.

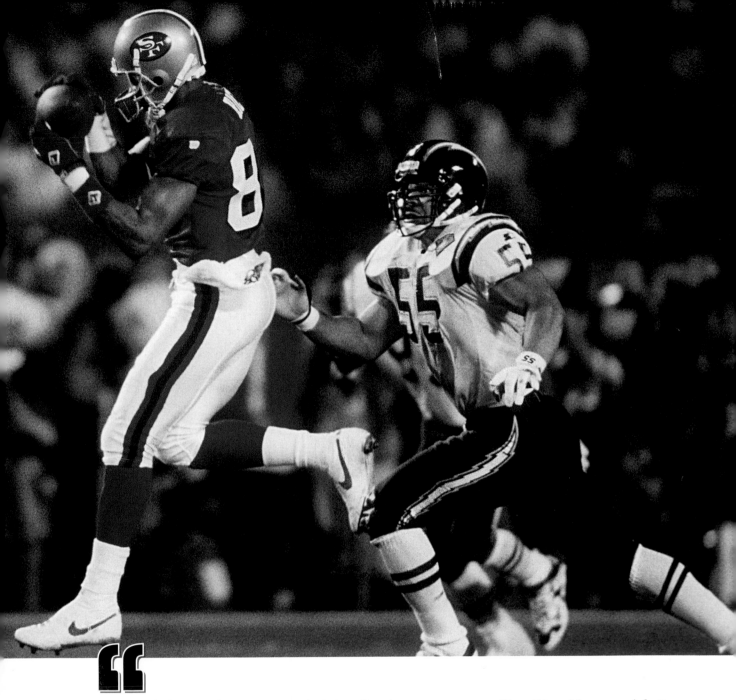

# "

# THIS IS NO STREAK, MAN. THIS IS WHAT WE DO."

—49ERS QUARTERBACK
**STEVE YOUNG** AFTER
SUPER BOWL XXIX, REFERRING TO
HIS TEAM'S WINNING 13 OF 14 GAMES
TO CLOSE OUT THE SEASON

San Francisco wasted no time showing why. The Niners began the game with the fastest scoring drive in Super Bowl history, as Young found Rice for a 44-yard touchdown 1:24 into the game.

Four quarters later, San Francisco had won 49–26. The 49ers became the first franchise to win five Super Bowls. Young set the game record for most touchdown passes (six), and Rice set career Super Bowl records for receiving yards (512), receptions (28), and TD catches (7). Rice also tied his own single-game Super Bowl record for TD receptions (3).

"Jerry Rice with one arm is better than everyone in the league with two arms," said Young after his favorite target, already an eight-time first-team All-Pro, caught 10 passes for 149 yards.

Young broke down crying after the game, then gave the postgame speech in the locker room, a task that usually falls to the coach. "There were times when this was hard! But this is the greatest feeling in the world!" he shouted. "No one—no one—can ever take this away from us! No one, ever! It's ours!"

# CHAPTER 2

# The ULTIMATE NFL DREAM TEAM

The best player at
every position

# OFFENSE

## 1 WIDE RECEIVER
# RANDY MOSS

MINNESOTA VIKINGS (1998–2004, 2010)
OAKLAND RAIDERS (2005–2006)
NEW ENGLAND PATRIOTS (2007–2010)
TENNESSEE TITANS (2010)
SAN FRANCISCO 49ERS (2012)

Nicknamed the Freak, Randy Moss could outrun, outjump, and outcatch anyone. As a rookie in 1998, Moss caught 17 touchdowns for the Minnesota Vikings, leading the NFL. Nine seasons later, Moss was still dominating when he set the single-season record for receiving touchdowns (23) with the New England Patriots.

## 2 TIGHT END
# TONY GONZALEZ

KANSAS CITY CHIEFS (1997–2008)
ATLANTA FALCONS (2009–2013)

Gonzalez played basketball in college and brought his hoops athleticism to the NFL, where he helped define the modern tight end—big, hard to cover, great hands. Gonzalez's 1,325 receptions rank second all time, and he is in the top 10 in receiving yards (15,127) and touchdowns (111).

## 3 OFFENSIVE TACKLE
# JONATHAN OGDEN

BALTIMORE RAVENS (1996–2007)

Jonathan Ogden is a big dude. During his playing days, he was listed at 6'9", 340 pounds. That mass allowed him to lay into defenders on rushing plays. During Ogden's career, Ravens running backs had seven 1,000-yard rushing seasons.

## 4 GUARD
# LARRY ALLEN

DALLAS COWBOYS (1995–2005)
SAN FRANCISCO 49ERS (2006–2007)

Despite playing the unglamorous position of offensive guard, Larry Allen stood out. Allen could bench-press more than 700 pounds. An 11-time Pro Bowler, Allen opened up huge holes for Dallas Cowboys running back Emmitt Smith, helping Smith eventually become the NFL's all-time leading rusher.

## 5 RUNNING BACK
# BARRY SANDERS

DETROIT LIONS (1989–1998)

Barry Sanders played 10 seasons for the Lions and rushed for at least 1,300 yards in nine of them. With his stutter steps and jukes, Sanders was a highlight waiting to happen. He ranks third all time with 15,269 career rushing yards.

## 6 RUNNING BACK
# JIM BROWN

CLEVELAND BROWNS (1957–1965)

Jim Brown was bigger, faster, and stronger than many of the defenders who tried to tackle him. Brown led the NFL in rushing in eight out of his nine pro seasons. He remains the only player to average at least 100 rushing yards per game for an entire career.

## 7 QUARTERBACK
# TOM BRADY

NEW ENGLAND PATRIOTS (2000–CURRENT)

Tom Brady idolized Joe Montana growing up. Few believed, however, that Brady would one day surpass his hero. Cool under pressure, just like Montana, Brady has played in eight Super Bowls. He has won five, which just happens to be one more than Montana.

## 8 CENTER
# BRUCE MATTHEWS

HOUSTON OILERS/TENNESSEE TITANS (1983–2001)

Bruce Matthews's father, brother, sons, and nephews are all current or former NFL players. But only Bruce had the technique, strength, and agility to play every O-line position. Matthews started 293 games, which was an NFL record before Brett Favre eclipsed him.

## 9 GUARD
# JOHN HANNAH

NEW ENGLAND PATRIOTS (1973–1985)

John Hannah's 33-inch thighs hinted at his tremendous lower-body strength. Hannah burst off the line of scrimmage and pushed defensive tackles around for 13 NFL seasons. In 1981, SPORTS ILLUSTRATED put him on the cover with the headline THE BEST OFFENSIVE LINEMAN OF ALL TIME.

## 10 OFFENSIVE TACKLE
# ANTHONY MUÑOZ

CINCINNATI BENGALS (1980–1992)

A nine-time All-Pro, Anthony Muñoz was the first Bengal enshrined in the Hall of Fame. As the anchor of Cincinnati's offensive line, he helped the Bengals lead the NFL in total rushing yards in back-to-back seasons (1988–1989). The reliable tackle played in 185 games over his 12-season career.

## 11 WIDE RECEIVER
# JERRY RICE

SAN FRANCISCO 49ERS (1985–2000)
OAKLAND RAIDERS (2001–2004)
SEATTLE SEAHAWKS (2004)

Jerry Rice is perhaps the only player in this G.O.A.T. book to actually be nicknamed the G.O.A.T. during his playing days. The stats back up the moniker. Rice holds the all-time records for total receiving yards (22,895), receiving touchdowns (197), and receptions (1,549).

## 1 CORNERBACK
### DARRELL GREEN
WASHINGTON REDSKINS (1983–2002)

Darrell Green, who played 20 seasons with the Redskins, never seemed to slow down. Just 5'9", the cornerback used his unrivaled acceleration to close on receivers and track down ballcarriers. The secret to his success? He claimed it was the Tootsie Rolls he stuck in his socks during games.

## 2 DEFENSIVE END
### BRUCE SMITH
BUFFALO BILLS (1985–1999)
WASHINGTON REDSKINS (2000–2003)

Bruce Smith is the only player to ever record at least 200 career sacks. He had a variety of moves that he used to juke his opponent and get to the quarterback. The eight-time All-Pro lineman was also strong against the run, twice making more than 100 tackles in a single season.

## 3 DEFENSIVE TACKLE
### MERLIN OLSEN
LOS ANGELES RAMS (1962–1976)

Big, strong, and technically sound, Merlin Olsen played inside on the Los Angeles Rams' Fearsome Foursome defensive line. Olsen clogged up the middle, freeing his linemates to get to the quarterback. The multitalented Olsen became a TV actor on shows such as *Little House on the Prairie* after his NFL career ended.

## 4 DEFENSIVE TACKLE
### JOE GREENE
PITTSBURGH STEELERS (1969–1981)

Joe Greene was a leader of Pittsburgh's famed Steel Curtain defense, which won four Super Bowls. "Mean Joe" was a five-time All-Pro and two-time Defensive Player of the Year who struck fear in opposing running backs, offensive linemen, and quarterbacks.

## 5 DEFENSIVE END
### REGGIE WHITE
PHILADELPHIA EAGLES (1985–1992)
GREEN BAY PACKERS (1993–1998)
CAROLINA PANTHERS (2000)

In 15 NFL seasons, White had 198 sacks, the second-most all time. Nicknamed the Minister of Defense, White overpowered opposing linemen on his way to becoming a 13-time Pro Bowler, eight-time All-Pro, and two-time Defensive Player of the Year.

## 6 LINEBACKER
### LAWRENCE TAYLOR
NEW YORK GIANTS (1981–1993)

Lawrence Taylor changed the way the position of linebacker was played. He is the only linebacker to ever win the NFL MVP award, which he did in 1986. The leader of the Giants' Big Blue Wrecking Crew defense, Taylor had 132½ sacks in his career.

## 7 LINEBACKER
### DICK BUTKUS
CHICAGO BEARS (1965–1973)

Dick Butkus met opposing ballcarriers with a bone-crunching thud. He was a turnover machine who recovered 27 fumbles and intercepted 22 passes in just 119 career games. Butkus won the Newspaper Enterprise Association's Defensive Player of the Year award in 1969 on a team that won one game.

## 8 LINEBACKER
### RAY LEWIS
BALTIMORE RAVENS (1996–2012)

Ray Lewis patrolled the middle of the field, anticipating plays and contributing to every aspect of the defense. A vocal leader on and off the field, Lewis helped the Ravens set the record for fewest points allowed (165), in 2000, the same season he was named Super Bowl MVP.

## 9 CORNERBACK
### DEION SANDERS
ATLANTA FALCONS (1989–1993)
SAN FRANCISCO 49ERS (1994)
DALLAS COWBOYS (1995–1999)
WASHINGTON REDSKINS (2000)
BALTIMORE RAVENS (2004–2005)

A two-sport athlete good enough to get 558 major league hits, Deion Sanders was also one of the most dominant cornerbacks in NFL history. The flashy Sanders returned nine interceptions, six punts, three kickoffs, and one fumble for touchdowns in 14 NFL seasons.

## 10 STRONG SAFETY
### TROY POLAMALU
PITTSBURGH STEELERS (2003–2014)

Instantly recognizable thanks to the curly hair overflowing his helmet, Troy Polamalu had a knack for incredible plays, intercepting passes with one hand or leaping over the entire offensive line to sack the quarterback. He returned 32 interceptions for 398 yards during his career.

## 11 FREE SAFETY
### RONNIE LOTT
SAN FRANCISCO 49ERS (1981–1990)
LOS ANGELES RAIDERS (1991–1992)
NEW YORK JETS (1993–1994)

Ronnie Lott was so versatile, he was named All-Pro as a free safety, strong safety, and cornerback at different points in his career. Lott was so driven, he once had the tip of his finger amputated after an on-field injury so that he would not miss any games.

# DEFENSE

# SPECIAL TEAMS

### 1 PUNTER
### RAY GUY

OAKLAND RAIDERS (1973–1981)
LOS ANGELES RAIDERS (1982–1986)

Guy is the only punter ever taken in the first round of the NFL draft. The Raiders selected him 23rd overall in 1973, and Guy rewarded the franchise with 14 years of booming punts. That led to another distinction: He is the only punter in the Hall of Fame.

### 2 KICK RETURNER
### GALE SAYERS

CHICAGO BEARS (1965–1971)

The same qualities that made Gale Sayers a great running back also made him an incredible returner. In only 68 games, he returned six kicks and two punts for touchdowns. In one game in 1965, he scored a record six TDs: four rushing, one receiving, and one on a punt return.

### 3 PUNT RETURNER
### DEVIN HESTER

CHICAGO BEARS (2006–2013)
ATLANTA FALCONS (2014–2015)
BALTIMORE RAVENS (2016)
SEATTLE SEAHAWKS (2016)

Devin Hester made teams regret kicking in his direction. As a rookie in 2006, he led the league in punt return yards (600) and punts returned for touchdowns (3). He returned the opening kickoff at Super Bowl XLI for a score and holds the all-time record for punt return TDs, with 14.

### 4 KICKER
### ADAM VINATIERI

NEW ENGLAND PATRIOTS (1996–2005)
INDIANAPOLIS COLTS (2006–CURRENT)

No kicker has come up bigger in big moments than Adam Vinatieri. He booted last-second game-winners for the New England Patriots in both Super Bowl XXXVI and XXXVIII. During his 22 NFL seasons through 2017, Vinatieri had made 39 field goals of at least 50 yards.

# BENCH

## 1 QUARTERBACK
### JOE MONTANA
SAN FRANCISCO 49ERS (1979–1992)
KANSAS CITY CHIEFS (1993–1994)

When the San Francisco 49ers drafted Joe Montana, coach Bill Walsh had found the perfect QB to run his West Coast offense. Nicknamed Joe Cool, Montana almost always made the smart play in pressure situations. He finished his career with four Super Bowl titles and two NFL MVP awards.

## 2 RUNNING BACK
### WALTER PAYTON
CHICAGO BEARS (1975–1987)

The player nicknamed Sweetness was a treat to watch. Walter Payton would beat defenders with power, speed, and moves. He rushed more than 300 times in 10 seasons and retired after 13 seasons as the NFL's all-time leading rusher (16,726 yards).

## 3 WIDE RECEIVER
### TERRELL OWENS
SAN FRANCISCO 49ERS (1996–2003)
PHILADELPHIA EAGLES (2004–2005)
DALLAS COWBOYS (2006–2008)
BUFFALO BILLS (2009)
CINCINNATI BENGALS (2010)

Terrell Owens once pulled a marker out of his sock and signed a football after a catch. But he was able to back up his antics with his play. A six-time Pro Bowler and five-time first-team All-Pro, Owens ranks behind only Jerry Rice with 15,934 career receiving yards.

## 4 DEFENSIVE END
### J.J. WATT
HOUSTON TEXANS (2011–CURRENT)

With unrivaled strength, J.J. Watt dominates offensive linemen one-on-one, often moving positions along the line to pick on different opponents. He is the only player in NFL history with multiple 20-sack seasons (2012, 2014).

## 5 DEFENSIVE BACK
### ROD WOODSON
PITTSBURGH STEELERS (1987–1996)
SAN FRANCISCO 49ERS (1997)
BALTIMORE RAVENS (1998–2001)
OAKLAND RAIDERS (2002–2003)

Few plays can swing the momentum in a football game faster than an interception or a punt return for a touchdown. Rod Woodson could do both. He finished his career with 12 interceptions returned for scores—an NFL record. He also returned two punts and two kicks for touchdowns.

## 6 LINEBACKER
### RAY NITSCHKE
GREEN BAY PACKERS (1958–1972)

Ray Nitschke was an indispensable member of coach Vince Lombardi's Green Bay Packers dynasty. Nitschke was so tough that when a steel observation tower fell on him at Packers practice, Lombardi told everyone to get back to work, knowing it would take more than that to stop his linebacker.

# CHAPTER 3

# The TOP 10 SINGLE-SEASON COLLEG

The greatest years for the most storied programs in history

E TEAMS

# #1

## 1995
# NEBRASKA
## Cornhuskers

**1** **Number of times** the Huskers trailed during the 1995 season. Nebraska was down 7–0 to Washington State but wound up winning by 14 points.

Center **Aaron Graham** was one of five co-captains on the 1995 Cornhuskers team.

His fellow co-captains were linebacker Phil Ellis, tight end Mark Gilman, defensive tackle Christian Peter, and safety Tony Veland. All five were fifth-year seniors. During their time with the program, Nebraska won five Big Eight Conference titles and two national championships, and went undefeated in three-straight regular seasons.

Despite winning the national championship the previous season, the Nebraska Cornhuskers entered 1995 ranked *second* in the country. Fine then. The Cornhuskers, who had lost only once in the previous two seasons, would just have to show everyone that they weren't planning on losing another game anytime in the near future.

While the Cornhuskers had things under control between the lines, things were more complicated off the field. Not even three weeks into the season, half a dozen players had been arrested. Nevertheless, though controversy surrounded the program, the Huskers just kept winning. Aside from a 35–21 "scare" against Washington State, they beat all other opponents by at least 23 points. Nebraska's average margin of victory during the regular season? A whopping 39 points.

The 1995 squad ranked first in the country in scoring (52.4 points per game) and rushing (399.8 yards) and was second in total offense (556.3).

The team's leader was quarterback Tommie Frazier, who played only four

**COACH**
Tom Osborne

**RECORD**
12–0

**1995 NATIONAL CHAMPIONS**

games in 1994 because of blood clots in his right leg. In 1995, however, he was spectacular. Frazier ran coach Tom Osborne's option offense with ease. Frazier threw for 1,362 yards and 17 touchdowns and was also the team's top scorer on the ground, with 14 rushing TDs.

Facing undefeated Florida in the Fiesta Bowl, Nebraska did more than just win: The Huskers scored 29 unanswered points and held Florida to zero yards of offense in the second quarter. By the end, Nebraska's defense had limited the Gators to –28 yards rushing and sacked QB Danny Wuerffel seven times. The final score was a lopsided 62–24.

Frazier, who finished second in the Heisman Trophy race, let voters know just what he thought about that decision with his play. He rushed for 199 yards and two scores and passed for 105 yards and a TD in the Fiesta Bowl.

"We physically outmuscled them," said Huskers defensive tackle Jason Peter. "We beat them down. We beat everybody down."

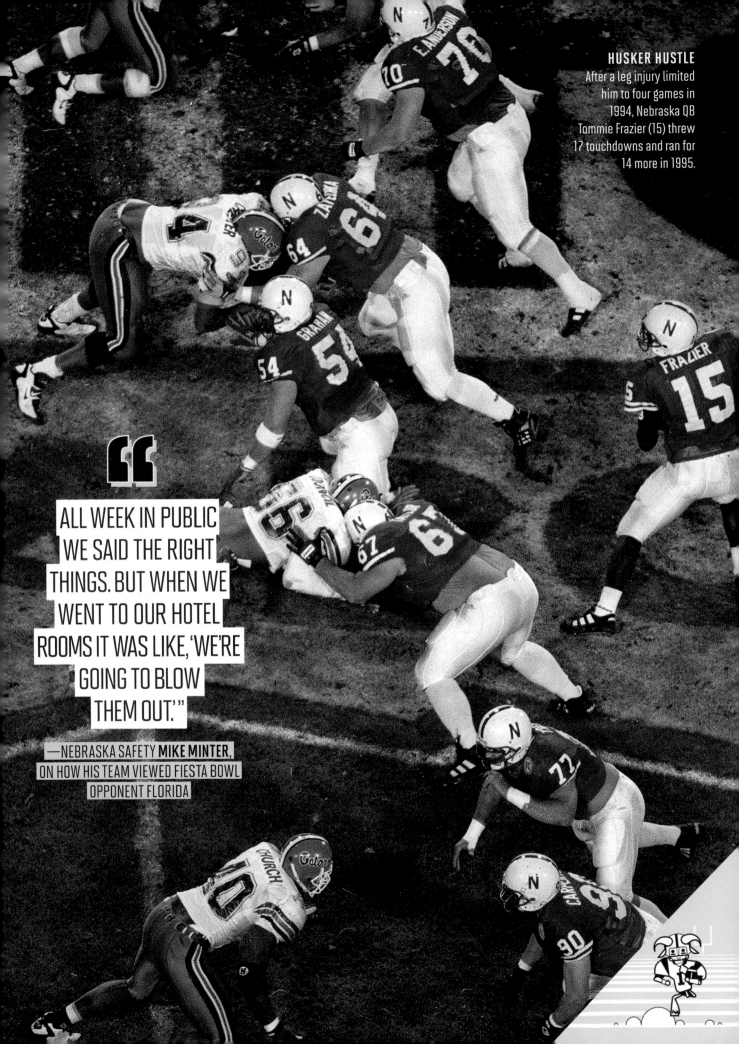

**HUSKER HUSTLE**
After a leg injury limited him to four games in 1994, Nebraska QB Tommie Frazier (15) threw 17 touchdowns and ran for 14 more in 1995.

" **ALL WEEK IN PUBLIC WE SAID THE RIGHT THINGS. BUT WHEN WE WENT TO OUR HOTEL ROOMS IT WAS LIKE, 'WE'RE GOING TO BLOW THEM OUT.' "**

—NEBRASKA SAFETY **MIKE MINTER**, ON HOW HIS TEAM VIEWED FIESTA BOWL OPPONENT FLORIDA

# #2

## 1972 USC *Trojans*

"*That's Not Thunder You Hear, It's USC.*" This was the headline of a SPORTS ILLUSTRATED story about the 1972 Trojans football team, and it perfectly summed up USC's dominance.

Through the first 10 games of the season, Southern Cal had beaten 10 teams—including four ranked in the top 20—by an average of 28.6 points per game. It was a remarkable accomplishment for a USC squad that had finished 6-4-1 in each of the previous two seasons.

The 1972 Trojans could run with tailback Anthony Davis. They could

**COACH**
John McKay

**RECORD**
12–0

**1972 NATIONAL CHAMPIONS**

pass with quarterback Mike Rae, targeting tight end Charles Young and wideout Lynn Swann. And they played exceptional defense, as they demonstrated in the 24–7 victory over Number 14 UCLA that motivated the SPORTS ILLUSTRATED headline.

That win over the rival Bruins meant the Trojans, top-ranked since the second week of the season, were 10–0 headed into another high-profile matchup, with Number 10 Notre Dame.

Davis put on a show against the Fighting Irish. He scored a school-record six touchdowns (four rushing, two on kick returns) in a 45–23 win. The victory earned USC a

trip to the Rose Bowl, where it would play third-ranked Ohio State.

The Trojans started slowly against the Buckeyes. At halftime, the score was 7–7. But once USC got going, it really got going. The team scored 35 points in the second half, winning the game 42–17.

Davis rushed for 157 yards and a score. Senior fullback Sam Cunningham set a Rose Bowl record with four touchdowns. Cunningham's bruising goal line play (three of his TDs came from the one-yard line; the fourth was from the two) earned him the game's MVP award.

Addressing his team's second-half turnaround, USC coach John McKay said matter-of-factly, "We didn't make any changes in strategy—we just kicked the pants off them."

---

### HUT, HUT, WHAT??

In 1972, USC left tackle **Pete Adams found a stray dog** who became a constant presence with the team. The *Los Angeles Times* said the dog could be seen "running wind sprints with the Trojans, eavesdropping on huddles, and cavorting in the locker room." Said assistant coach Craig Fertig, "It's our mascot. Its formal name is Cosmo."

### BIG G.O.A.T. ON CAMPUS

Because freshmen weren't allowed to play, sophomore running back **Anthony Davis** began the 1972 season third on the USC depth chart. Even though he did not get his first start until the eighth game of the season, Davis still ran for 1,323 yards and 17 touchdowns. It was the first of three 1,000-yard seasons for Davis, who finished second in Heisman Trophy voting in 1974.

**RING OF FIRE**
In 1972, USC quarterback Mike Rae (6) was surrounded by weapons on offense, including running back Anthony Davis (28) and receiver Lynn Swann (22).

**#3**

**1945**

# ARMY

## Black Knights

World War II had barely ended when Army played its first game of the 1945 season. With so much attention having been paid to the boys "over there" who were fighting, the country was only too happy to turn its focus to the boys who were lighting up gridiron scoreboards.

Army averaged a record 56.0 points per game in 1944, then scored an NCAA-best 45.8 per game in 1945. Halfback Glenn Davis and fullback Felix (Doc) Blanchard were known as Mr. Outside and Mr. Inside, respectively, for the ways they ran past the defensive line. With the dual-threat backfield and a stingy defense, the Cadets (so nicknamed because Army is a military academy) rolled over their opponents. They had five shutouts, and the other four teams they played only managed to score an average of 11.5 points.

Blanchard was the 1945 NCAA scoring champion. He had 19 touchdowns and booted one extra point to help him win the Heisman Trophy. (Davis would win his

Heisman the following season.) In addition to his rushing duties, Blanchard was Army's kicker and also played defense. (The NCAA changed its substitution rules in 1941, but having players who played offense or defense exclusively had not yet become the norm.)

In addition to playing both ways, Blanchard also played other sports. He was a sprinter and shot-putter on the track team. Davis, meanwhile, played baseball for three seasons, basketball for one, and ran track.

"[They] were both easy to block for," Army tackle Tex Coulter recalled years later. "You didn't really need to get in a solid lick, because they had this sense of where to go, that great running instinct."

The service academies did not play in bowl games at the time, so the Cadets' outstanding season ended with a 32–13 win in the all-important Army-Navy game. In the finale, Davis rushed for two scores, and Blanchard rushed for three and intercepted a pass. That victory was enough for Army to retain the top ranking.

**COACH**
Red Blaik

**RECORD**
9–0

**1945 NATIONAL CHAMPIONS**

DOUBLE TROUBLE
Army's dynamic rushing duo of Glenn Davis (41) and Felix (Doc) Blanchard (35) were known for their complementary running styles.

"

I DOUBT IF ANY TEAM EVER HAD TWO SUCH PLAYERS IN THE BACKFIELD AT THE SAME TIME."

—ARMY COACH **RED BLAIK** OF HIS TALENTED DUO, FULLBACK DOC BLANCHARD AND HALFBACK GLENN DAVIS

**BEARING DOWN**
With defensive backs Ed Reed (20) and Phillip Buchanon patrolling the field, teams thought twice about throwing against the Hurricanes.

# 2001
# MIAMI
## *Hurricanes*

### PLAYBOOK INSIDER

With five minutes to go in the final game of the regular season, Virginia Tech trailed Miami 26–24. The Hokies had the ball at midfield with a chance to spoil Miami's perfect season. But Hurricanes safety **Ed Reed** wasn't going to let that happen. He made a diving interception with 4:24 left, and Miami's offense was able to eat up enough clock and hold on for victory.

### BIG G.O.A.T. ON CAMPUS

By the end of the 2001 season, Miami QB **Ken Dorsey** was already 26–1 as a starter. He finished third in the Heisman voting in 2001, then led Miami to 12 straight wins in 2002. (The Hurricanes lost to Ohio State in the Fiesta Bowl.)

The 2000 Hurricanes went 11–1 and finished second in the polls. So expectations were high heading into 2001. But then Miami coach Butch Davis took an NFL job two days before high school seniors could officially commit to a college. The storied program was suddenly without a leader.

But Miami didn't have to look far to find one. The Hurricanes promoted offensive coordinator Larry Coker to become head coach. His system had already proved effective for QB Ken Dorsey. After becoming head coach, Coker helped Miami run the table and win the national championship. From September 10, 2000, through January 3, 2003, Miami did not lose a football game.

In the early 2000s, Miami teams were not as brash as the squads that won national titles in the 1980s and early 1990s. The 2001 Hurricanes were content to let their play speak for them. "We have a lot of quiet, easygoing guys like me, who leave it all on the field," said linebacker Jonathan Vilma. "People talk at us, and we listen and say, 'That's nice.

**COACH**
Larry
Coker

**RECORD**
12–0

**2001 NATIONAL CHAMPIONS**

Now look at the scoreboard.' "

Only twice that season did the scoreboard indicate a winning margin of victory for Miami that was less than 22 points: against Boston College (18–7 in the eighth game) and Virginia Tech (26–24 in the final game of the regular season).

On the ground, Clinton Portis (1,200 yards) led the charge, and Frank Gore (562) and Willis McGahee (314) pitched in. Dorsey's favorite aerial targets were tight end Jeremy Shockey (40 catches, 519 yards, seven TDs) and Andre Johnson (37 catches, 362 yards, 10 TDs). All, with the exception of Dorsey, would go on to become impact players in the pros.

Miami was so dominant that the national title game, which was played in the Rose Bowl, was essentially over before halftime. The Hurricanes went up 34–0 against Nebraska and then hit cruise control on their way to a 37–14 victory.

Said Cornhuskers coach Frank Solich afterward, "There's a reason why only one team in the country is undefeated."

# 1974
# OKLAHOMA
## *Sooners*

**#5**

## STATS INCREDIBLE!

**5**

**Touchdowns** that Oklahoma, down 13–10, scored in a 7½-minute period beginning late in the third quarter against Oklahoma State in the final game of the season. The Sooners won 44–13.

## PLAYBOOK INSIDER

Oklahoma's hopes of going undefeated were in doubt against 17th-ranked Texas. The Longhorns had the ball on the Oklahoma 18-yard line late in the fourth quarter with a chance to tie or take the lead. But the Sooners' defense forced a fumble that was recovered by All-America tackle **Lee Roy Selmon.** Oklahoma held on for a 16–13 victory and improved its record to 4–0.

t might have been the greatest season no one saw. In the spring of 1973, the NCAA placed Oklahoma on probation for recruiting violations. In addition to forfeiting eight of its 1972 wins and being banned from the postseason in 1973 and 1974, the Sooners couldn't appear on television in 1974 and 1975.

Rather than sulking, new head coach Barry Switzer and his team made the most of the situation in 1973. Switzer even thought the penalties provided a little extra motivation. "How else can you explain the fact that a team that was picked for no better than fourth in the conference went 10-0-1 and ended up Number 3 in the country? Something else beside talent and coaching snuck in there," he said.

The 1974 season was more of the same, only better. OU's wishbone offense was a three-pronged ground-focused attack. Running back Joe Washington (1,321 yards), fullback Jim Littrell (837), and quarterback Steve Davis (659) helped the Sooners average an NCAA-best 43.0 points per game. The tough Oklahoma defense did not allow a single team to score more than 14 points all season.

The United Press International poll refused to recognize the Sooners because they were on probation. But the Associated Press poll voters made 8–0 Oklahoma the Number 1 team in the country after top-ranked Ohio State lost.

The Sooners didn't let the top ranking slip from their grasp.

Oklahoma trounced Kansas 45–14 the following week to set up a showdown with conference foe Nebraska, the country's sixth-ranked team. Even without completing a pass, the Sooners' offense rolled. Oklahoma finished with 482 rushing yards and won 28–14.

The Sooners closed out the regular season with a win over Oklahoma State. Even without a bowl game appearance, Oklahoma received 51 of 60 first-place votes in the AP poll to retain its Number 1 ranking. (USC, which beat Ohio State in the Rose Bowl, was Number 1 in the UPI poll.)

It would have been an impressive accomplishment without the probation. But the obstacles that Oklahoma had to overcome in 1974 made it a season for the ages.

**COACH**
Barry Switzer

**RECORD**
11–0

**1974 AP NATIONAL CHAMPIONS**

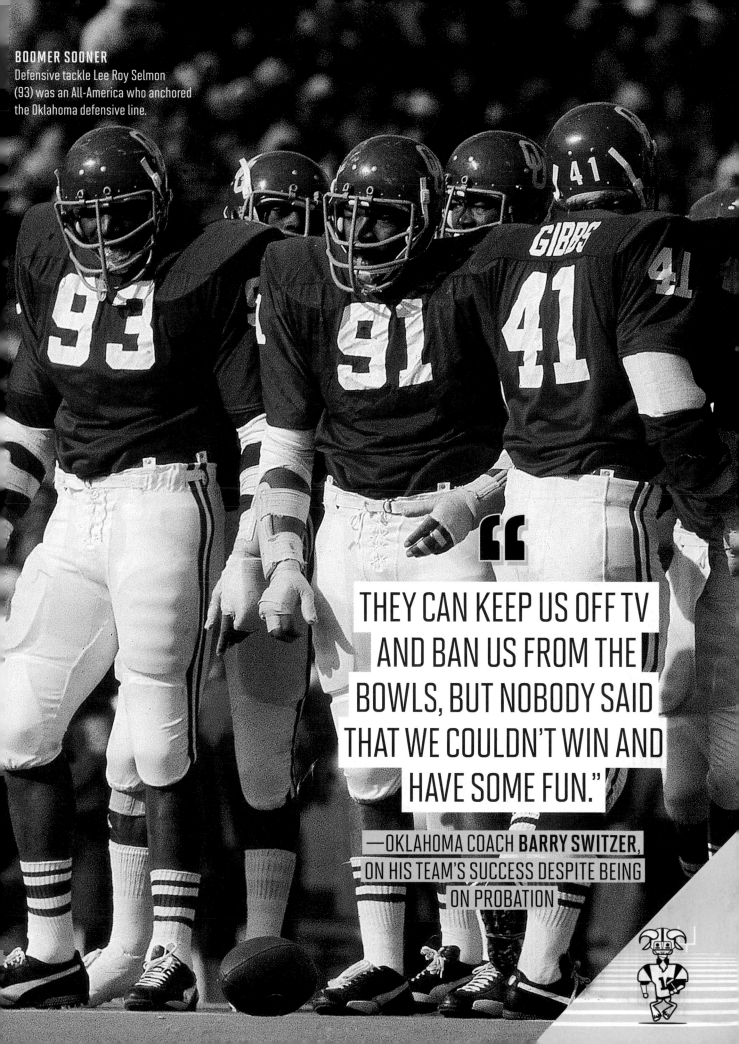

**BOOMER SOONER**
Defensive tackle Lee Roy Selmon (93) was an All-America who anchored the Oklahoma defensive line.

"

THEY CAN KEEP US OFF TV AND BAN US FROM THE BOWLS, BUT NOBODY SAID THAT WE COULDN'T WIN AND HAVE SOME FUN."

—OKLAHOMA COACH **BARRY SWITZER**, ON HIS TEAM'S SUCCESS DESPITE BEING ON PROBATION

## 1979
# ALABAMA
## *Crimson Tide*

The Crimson Tide were indeed rolling heading into 1979. Alabama had gone 22–2 over the past two seasons and was the AP national champion in 1978. (USC was the UPI poll champion.) The Tide started 1979 ranked second in the country and were focused on winning another title.

Blowouts became the norm for Alabama. The Crimson Tide averaged 31.9 points and allowed just 5.2. The team dominated in every aspect of the game. The defense hauled in a school-record 25 interceptions. The offense, meanwhile, set a school record for most first downs per game (23.9).

**COACH**
Bear Bryant

**RECORD**
12–0

**1979 NATIONAL CHAMPIONS**

By the middle of October, the Crimson Tide were atop the AP poll.

Alabama had its traditional regular-season finale against in-state rival Auburn. At the time, the Tigers were ranked 14th. The undefeated Tide did not play their finest game—they lost four fumbles in the third quarter—and trailed 18–17 with 12 minutes to go in the fourth. But quarterback Steadman Shealy drove the team 82 yards for a touchdown. Alabama won 25–18. "I had a good feeling during that drive," said Shealy. "I felt like we could do it if we stuck to our knittin'."

It was a win, but the team fell to Number 2, as Ohio State took over the top spot. In the Sugar Bowl against sixth-ranked Arkansas, the Tide showed why they deserved to be Number 1. Running backs Major Ogilvie (67 yards rushing, two touchdowns) and Billy Jackson (120 yards on only 13 carries) moved the football on offense. Alabama's D held the Razorbacks to zero net yards on six third downs in the first half. A 17–3 halftime lead turned into a 24–9 Alabama victory.

Immediately afterward, the Tide players found TV sets to watch top-ranked Ohio State play Number 3 USC in the Rose Bowl. The Trojans beat the Buckeyes, leaving Alabama as the nation's only unbeaten team. (USC had one tie.) When it was all over, voters in both polls ranked the Crimson Tide Number 1.

### HUT, HUT, WHAT??

After eight games in 1979, Alabama was one of six unbeaten teams, along with Nebraska, USC, Houston, Ohio State, and Florida State. While their styles of play were different, there was something that tied the teams together: **They all wore some shade of red.**

### UNSUNG HERO

Kicker **Alan McElroy** set an Alabama single-season record with 15 field goals made. He scored the only points in a 3–0 victory over LSU on a rainy November night. With 15 field goals and 32 extra points, McElroy scored 77 points, second in the SEC.

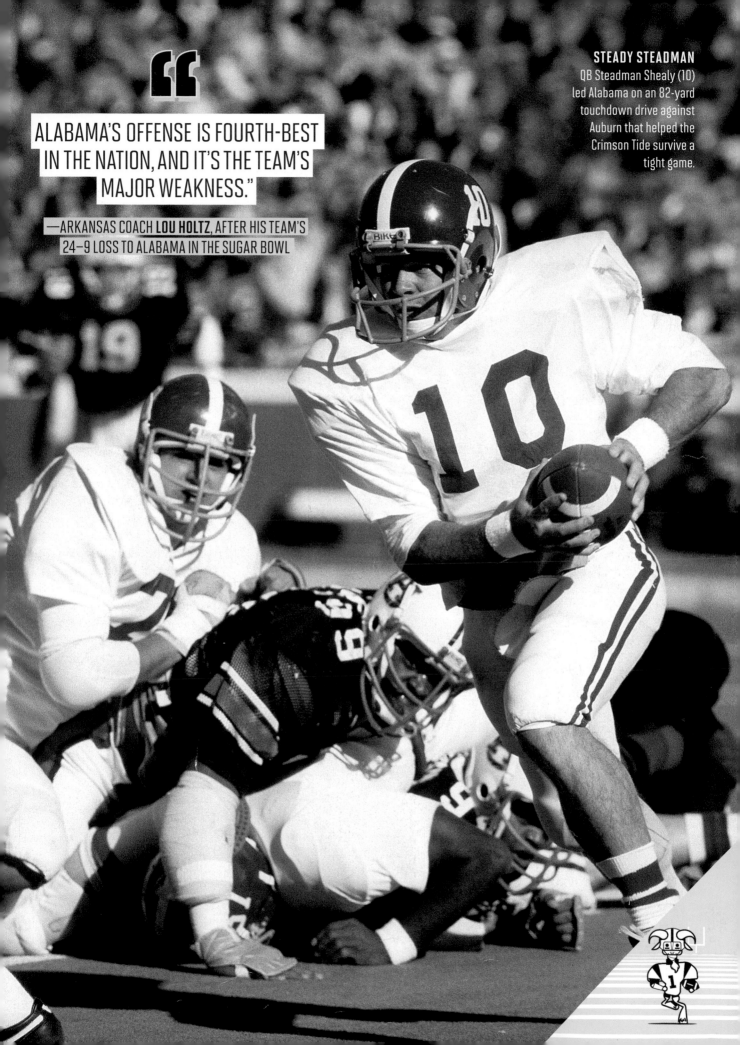

"

ALABAMA'S OFFENSE IS FOURTH-BEST IN THE NATION, AND IT'S THE TEAM'S MAJOR WEAKNESS."

—ARKANSAS COACH **LOU HOLTZ**, AFTER HIS TEAM'S 24–9 LOSS TO ALABAMA IN THE SUGAR BOWL

**STEADY STEADMAN**
QB Steadman Shealy (10) led Alabama on an 82-yard touchdown drive against Auburn that helped the Crimson Tide survive a tight game.

**LISTEN UP**
Notre Dame coach Frank
Leahy (center) led the
Fighting Irish to a second-straight
undefeated season in 1947.

# #7

## 1947
# NOTRE DAME
## *Fighting Irish*

The Notre Dame team that didn't lose in 1946 lost only three starters to graduation. "We should be in very good shape next season," an uncharacteristically optimistic coach Frank Leahy said in March 1947. That was an understatement.

TIME magazine called the 1947 Fighting Irish team a "powerhouse." They certainly looked like one in their first game, a 40–6 win over Pittsburgh. The next week? Not so much. Practices had been brutal; players were worn down. The Irish beat Purdue 22–7, but the Boilermakers outgained them 128 to 89 yards on the ground. Notre Dame quarterback Johnny Lujack won the game through the air, completing 14 passes.

Team captain George Connor talked to Coach Leahy about letting up on the team during the week. "Leahy wound up cutting back on the practices, and it saved our season," halfback Terry Brennan recalled years later. Three games came and went before another team scored even a single point against the Fighting Irish.

**COACH**
Frank Leahy

**RECORD**
9–0

**1947 NATIONAL CHAMPIONS**

Notre Dame did not play in bowl games at the time, so the season's final game was against Southern California in the L.A. Coliseum.

The train trip west was a fruitful one. Lujack, who had already won the Heisman Trophy, ran an offense that outgained USC 461 yards to 173. Lujack even made an interception on defense as the Irish closed out a second-straight undefeated season with a 38–7 win.

Said Leahy to reporters, "I think that that was perhaps the best single game a Notre Dame team has ever played."

After the season, the Fighting Irish were voted national champions over another undefeated squad, from Michigan. Nine players on the 1947 Notre Dame team were All-America at some point, and seven would be elected to the College Football Hall of Fame. In addition to Lujack's Heisman win in 1947, end Leon Hart would go on to win the award in 1949, further testament that this was indeed a powerhouse team.

**2005**

# TEXAS
## *Longhorns*

**PLAYBOOK INSIDER**

Leading 38–33 with fewer than three minutes to go in the national title game, USC faced fourth-and-two near midfield and decided to go for it. Texas's defense stuffed Trojans running back LenDale White, giving Longhorns QB Vince Young time to orchestrate the winning drive.

**UNSUNG HERO**

Vince Young was a playmaker, but one of the reasons he had so much success at Texas, during the national title run in particular, was his offensive line. Left tackle **Jonathan Scott** protected Young's blind side, earning consensus All-America honors as a senior in 2005.

Texas won two national titles in the 1960s, but by the 2005 season, the Longhorns were looking at a 36-season championship drought.

It would take Vince Young, a confident, supremely talented quarterback, to end it. As a redshirt freshman in 2003, Young was 6–1 as a starter. In 2004, he became the first Texas player to pass and rush for at least 1,000 yards, as the Longhorns finished 11–1.

By 2005, Young and the Longhorns were ready to dominate. Texas began the season ranked second in the AP poll. It didn't take long for the Longhorns to get a big win. Texas beat fourth-ranked Ohio State 25–22 in Week 2. From then on, the Longhorns did not score fewer than 40 points and held opponents to an average of 16.2 per game. In the Big 12 title game, they defeated Colorado 70–3.

Young rushed for 1,050 yards and 12 touchdowns and passed for 3,036 yards and 26 TDs in 2005. Texas had other offensive weapons too. Running backs Jamaal Charles, Ramonce Taylor, Henry Melton, and Selvin Young combined

for 2,284 rushing yards and 41 TDs. Young's favorite target through the air was tight end David Thomas (613 yards, five TDs).

But Texas was still ranked second headed into the national title game at the Rose Bowl against USC. Fortunately, Young saved his best for last. He completed 30 of 40 passes for 267 yards and rushed 19 times for 200 yards and three TDs. With 6:42 left in the game and Texas down by 12, he carried the team on his back, including running for the winning score on fourth-and-five with 19 seconds remaining.

Texas's 41–38 victory over USC was particularly sweet for Young, who had finished second to Trojans running back Reggie Bush in the Heisman Trophy voting.

"I think you like that piece of crystal a little better, don't you?" announcer John Saunders asked Young after the QB accepted his offensive MVP award.

"That crystal's so beautiful," said Young. "And it's coming home to Texas. It's coming home all the way to Austin, Texas, baby!"

**COACH**
Mack Brown

**RECORD**
13–0

**2005 NATIONAL CHAMPIONS**

**HOOK 'EM**
Quarterback Vince Young (10) scored the game-winning touchdown in the national championship game with only 19 seconds remaining.

"WE KEPT OUR POISE, PUT THE BALL IN VINCE'S HANDS, AND LET THE MAN DO WHAT HE DOES."

—TEXAS RIGHT TACKLE **JUSTIN BLALOCK**, ON QB VINCE YOUNG'S THRILLING ROSE BOWL PERFORMANCE

**THE TEBOW SHOW**
Florida QB Tim Tebow (15) helped the Gators bounce back from a midseason loss and win the national championship.

# 2008
# FLORIDA
## *Gators*

The first two years of Tim Tebow's college career were eventful. As a freshman backup quarterback for Florida in 2006, he was the second-leading rusher on a team that won the national championship. The following year, he passed for 3,286 yards and 32 touchdowns, rushed for 895 yards and 23 scores, and became the first sophomore to win the Heisman Trophy.

So expectations were high at the start of 2008. The fifth-ranked Florida Gators looked ready to contend for another national title. It wouldn't be easy. There were three other Southeastern Conference teams that were also in the top 10. The season began swimmingly for the Gators. They were 3–0 heading into a matchup with unranked Ole Miss. Florida lost a heartbreaker 31–30, but it might have been the best thing to happen to the team. Afterward, Tebow delivered an emotional apology for the loss at his press conference. "You will never see any player in the entire country play as hard as I will play the

**COACH**
Urban Meyer

**RECORD**
13–1

**2008 NATIONAL CHAMPIONS**

rest of the season," he promised. "You will never see a team play harder than we will the rest of the season."

Florida did not lose another game. After dropping to 12th in the AP poll, the Gators crept up in the rankings, all the way to Number 2. The SEC championship game pitted second-ranked Florida against Number 1 Alabama. Tebow led the Gators to a fourth-quarter, come-from-behind victory (a career first) as Florida won 31–20.

The following weekend, Tebow missed out on a second Heisman award. Although Tebow received the most first-place votes, Oklahoma QB Sam Bradford had a higher overall vote total and won the trophy. But Tebow had the last laugh a month later when Florida faced Oklahoma in the Bowl Championship Series title game. Tebow threw for 231 yards, ran for 109 more, and was named the offensive MVP as the Gators won 24–14. Tebow had made good on his promise, and Florida had become one of the greatest college teams ever.

# 1968
# OHIO STATE
## *Buckeyes*

**#10**

The NCAA didn't allow freshmen to play varsity football until 1972, so at the dawn of the 1968 season, the buzz in Columbus, Ohio, was all about the Ohio State Buckeyes' sophomores: How super would they be?

By the time Ohio State hosted archrival Michigan in the final game of the regular season, five sophomores were starting on offense, and five started on defense. Among them was Rex Kern, the quarterback whom Buckeyes coach Woody Hayes trusted enough to call some of the plays. Kern threw for 972 yards, and his top four receivers, led by Bruce Jankowski and

**COACH**
Woody
Hayes

**RECORD**
10–0

**1968 NATIONAL CHAMPIONS**

Larry Zelina, were all sophomores.

On defense, the second-year stars were Jack Tatum, the intimidating cornerback who would go on to have a Pro Bowl career in the NFL, and middle guard Jim Stillwagon, who would win the Lombardi Trophy (as the nation's best player) and the Outland Trophy (best interior lineman) in 1970. Tatum, Stillwagon, and their defensive teammates shut out top-ranked Purdue in the third game of the season, a pivotal 13–0 win.

The centerpiece of the rushing attack, however, was a junior, fullback Jim Otis. He led Ohio State with 985 yards on the ground and 17 touchdowns. Against fourth-ranked Michigan, he rushed for 143 yards and four TDs as the Number 2 Buckeyes won 50–14. The victory propelled Ohio State to the top spot in the rankings and punched its ticket to the Rose Bowl.

The Buckeyes' opponent was mighty Southern California and Heisman Trophy winner O.J. Simpson, who tore off an 80-yard scoring run to help USC go up 10–0. "I told the guys in the huddle that we better get rolling and quit messing around," said Kern.

They did. In the end, the Buckeyes had the stouter defense, the better quarterback, and the edge in the turnover battle. They won 27–16, a victorious end to a truly super season.

## PLAYBOOK INSIDER

Holding a slim lead over USC in the Rose Bowl, Ohio State QB Rex Kern stepped in and took over. First, Kern rushed to the USC four-yard line. Then he used his arm to seal the win. Wrote SPORTS ILLUSTRATED's Dan Jenkins, "He faked the middle, rolled to his left, and threw a perfect little pass to Leophus Hayden, his halfback, who had sneaked lonesomely into the left-hand corner of the end zone."

## BIG G.O.A.T. ON CAMPUS

Red-headed **Rex Kern** suffered an ankle sprain, nearly fractured his jaw, endured muscle spasms in his back, and was knocked out twice in 1968. During the Rose Bowl, he dislocated his left shoulder but popped it back in. "There is never any doubt in Rex's mind that he can do anything," said one OSU assistant coach.

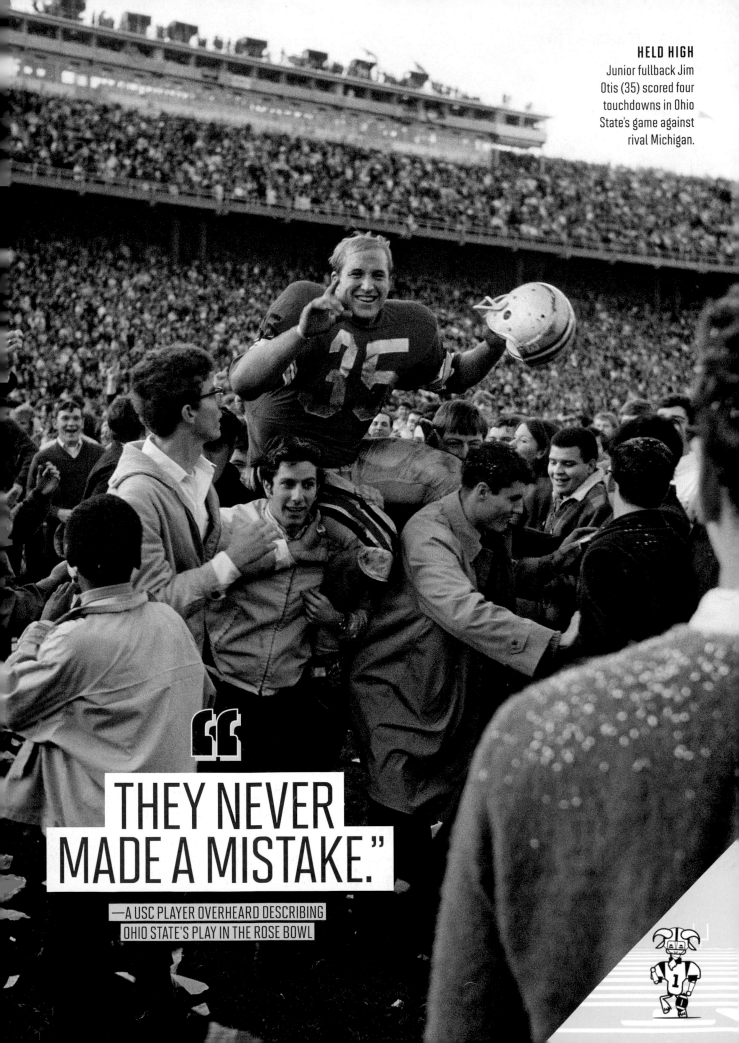

# " THEY NEVER MADE A MISTAKE. "

— A USC PLAYER OVERHEARD DESCRIBING OHIO STATE'S PLAY IN THE ROSE BOWL

# CHAPTER 4

# The BEST SEASON

## FOR EVERY NFL FRANCHISE

Find out more about the greatest year for your favorite team

### 2000 BALTIMORE RAVENS

Led by Hall of Fame linebacker Ray Lewis (52), Baltimore's defense allowed the fewest points (165) over a 16-game schedule, in 2000. In four playoff games, Baltimore gave up 23 points, including a lone touchdown in the Ravens' Super Bowl XXXV victory.

## 1998 ATLANTA FALCONS

Behind running back Jamal Anderson, the Falcons reached the Super Bowl for the first time in franchise history in 1998. Anderson rushed for a career-high 14 touchdowns, and his Dirty Bird celebration made him a fan favorite.

## 1947 ARIZONA CARDINALS

Before they ended up in Arizona (after a stop in St. Louis), the Cardinals played in Chicago. And in 1947, they played very well. Led by halfback Charley Trippi (far left), the team went 9–3 and defeated the Philadelphia Eagles in the NFL Championship Game.

## 2015 CAROLINA PANTHERS

Quarterback Cam Newton (1) and the Panthers had plenty of reason to celebrate after going 15–1 in 2015. Newton was the NFL MVP, and the Panthers made it to Super Bowl 50, the franchise's second championship game appearance.

## 1990 BUFFALO BILLS

On January 27, 1991, the Bills made the first of four consecutive Super Bowl appearances, a feat that has never been repeated. Although they lost each title game, the Bills still had a dominant offense, especially in 1990, led by running back Thurman Thomas (34) and quarterback Jim Kelly (12).

## 1985 CHICAGO BEARS

It all came together for the Bears in 1985. Chicago's famed 46 defense featured rookie tackle William (the Refrigerator) Perry, who recorded five sacks, as well as veterans like Mike Singletary and Richard Dent.

## 1988 CINCINNATI BENGALS

With running back Ickey Woods, Cincinnati finished 12–4 and went to the Super Bowl for just the second time in franchise history. Woods also developed one of the greatest touchdown celebrations ever, the Ickey Shuffle.

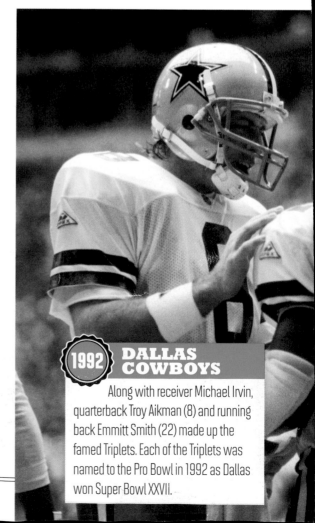

## 1992 DALLAS COWBOYS

Along with receiver Michael Irvin, quarterback Troy Aikman (8) and running back Emmitt Smith (22) made up the famed Triplets. Each of the Triplets was named to the Pro Bowl in 1992 as Dallas won Super Bowl XXVII.

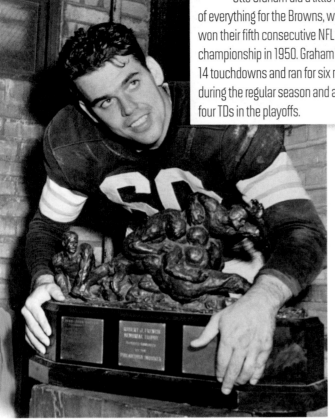

## 1950 CLEVELAND BROWNS

Otto Graham did a little bit of everything for the Browns, who won their fifth consecutive NFL championship in 1950. Graham threw 14 touchdowns and ran for six more during the regular season and added four TDs in the playoffs.

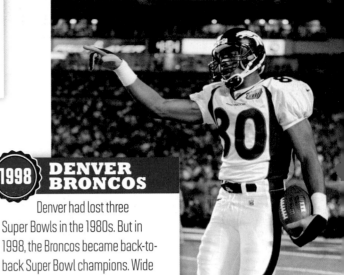

## 1998 DENVER BRONCOS

Denver had lost three Super Bowls in the 1980s. But in 1998, the Broncos became back-to-back Super Bowl champions. Wide receiver Rod Smith helped the Broncos win Super Bowl XXXIII with an 80-yard touchdown catch.

## 1953 DETROIT LIONS

It's been more than 25 years since the Lions won a playoff game, but in 1953 Detroit won its second consecutive NFL championship. Quarterback Bobby Layne (22) led the Lions in their 17–16 win over the Cleveland Browns in the championship game.

## 1962 GREEN BAY PACKERS

The Packers are one of the NFL's most storied franchises. Among all the great years, 1962 stands out. Quarterback Bart Starr (15) led the Packers to a near-perfect season. Green Bay finished 13–1 and won its second-straight NFL championship.

**2012 HOUSTON TEXANS**

The Texans played their first game in 2002. By 2012, Houston had finished 12–4 and advanced to the second round of the playoffs. Defensive end J.J. Watt was named Defensive Player of the Year after leading the NFL with 20½ sacks.

**1969 KANSAS CITY CHIEFS**

Quarterback Len Dawson injured his knee in the second game of 1969, but he didn't let that stop him from leading the Chiefs to the franchise's only Super Bowl victory. Dawson finished the season with the NFL's highest completion percentage (59.0).

**1999 JACKSONVILLE JAGUARS**

The Jaguars had been playing for only four years when they shocked the NFL by going 14–2 and reaching the AFC championship game in 1999. Jacksonville's offense was led by receiver Jimmy Smith, who caught 116 passes.

## 1968 INDIANAPOLIS COLTS

Despite losing in Super Bowl III, the 1968 Colts, who played in Baltimore at the time, are still remembered as one of the NFL's best teams. They finished 13–1 behind quarterback Earl Morrall (15) and his league-leading 26 touchdown passes.

## 1999 LOS ANGELES RAMS

Before moving to Los Angeles, the Rams built the Greatest Show on Turf in St. Louis. With quarterback Kurt Warner, the Rams scored at least 30 points in 12 games. Linebacker Mike Jones (52) stopped Kevin Dyson short of the end zone to secure a Super Bowl XXXIV victory.

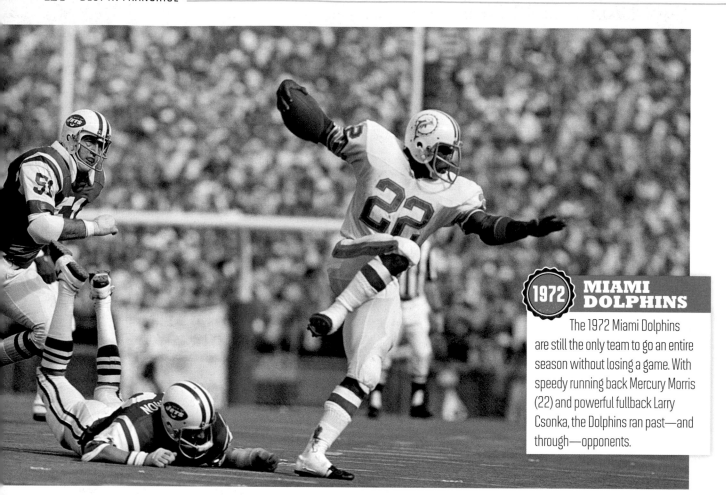

### 1972 MIAMI DOLPHINS

The 1972 Miami Dolphins are still the only team to go an entire season without losing a game. With speedy running back Mercury Morris (22) and powerful fullback Larry Csonka, the Dolphins ran past—and through—opponents.

### 1998 MINNESOTA VIKINGS

The Vikings had the best record in franchise history in 1998, finishing 15–1. With quarterback Randall Cunningham (7) and Hall of Fame receivers Cris Carter (80) and Randy Moss (84), Minnesota scored 556 points, an NFL record at the time.

## 2007 NEW ENGLAND PATRIOTS

With quarterback Tom Brady (12) and receiver Randy Moss (81) setting touchdown records, the Patriots went undefeated during the regular season in 2007. They lost in Super Bowl XLII, erasing hopes of a perfect season, but were still one of the best teams ever.

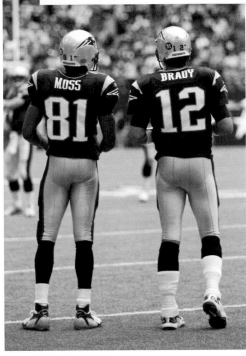

## 1986 NEW YORK GIANTS

Lawrence Taylor (56) is regarded as the greatest linebacker of all time. In 1986, he showed why. Taylor had 20½ sacks, the seventh-most all time, and led the Giants to a Super Bowl victory.

## 2009 NEW ORLEANS SAINTS

Just four seasons after the team and city suffered through Hurricane Katrina, quarterback Drew Brees and the Saints lifted New Orleans by going 13–3 and winning the franchise's first Super Bowl.

**1968**   **NEW YORK JETS**

The Jets pulled off one of the greatest upsets ever in Super Bowl III. New York was an 18-point underdog against the Baltimore Colts. But Jets quarterback Joe Namath guaranteed a victory before the game and delivered. New York won 16–7.

**2017**   **PHILADELPHIA EAGLES**

The Eagles had never won a Super Bowl. But that all changed in Super Bowl LII, thanks to quarterback Nick Foles (9). Foles threw three touchdowns and even caught one as the Eagles defeated the favored New England Patriots.

**1976** ## OAKLAND RAIDERS

The Raiders won Super Bowl XI after the 1976 season. It was the team's first and only championship. Oakland benefited from the elusive moves of QB Ken Stabler (12) and a strong running game.

**1963** ## SAN DIEGO CHARGERS

The Chargers won the only championship in franchise history in 1963. With Hall of Fame receiver Lance Alworth (19), San Diego's high-flying offense put up a lot of points, including 51 in the title game.

**1978** ## PITTSBURGH STEELERS

The Steelers dominated in the 1970s, winning four Super Bowls. But the 1978 squad was the best of the bunch. With defensive tackle "Mean" Joe Greene, Pittsburgh allowed just 195 points all season and won Super Bowl XIII.

**1989** **SAN FRANCISCO 49ERS**
Quarterback Joe Montana (16) guided the 49ers to their second consecutive Super Bowl in 1989. San Francisco had the NFL's best record (14–2), led the league in offense, and ranked third in defense.

**2013** **SEATTLE SEAHAWKS**
With Russell Wilson (right) and Marshawn Lynch running the offense and its Legion of Boom defense, the Seahawks went 13–3 in 2013 and won their first-ever Super Bowl.

## 2002 TAMPA BAY BUCCANEERS

The 2002 Bucs' defense is one of the all-time greats. It was at its best in Super Bowl XXXVII, when Tampa Bay returned three interceptions for touchdowns, including a 44-yard pick six from linebacker Derrick Brooks.

## 1991 WASHINGTON REDSKINS

The 1991 Redskins weren't flashy, but that didn't stop them from scoring the second-most points in franchise history (485) and winning Super Bowl XXVI. Washington got a boost on special teams from Brian Mitchell, who returned two punts for touchdowns.

## 1999 TENNESSEE TITANS

After changing its name from Oilers to Titans, Tennessee had a season to remember in 1999. The Titans pulled off the Music City Miracle in the playoffs when Kevin Dyson (87) returned a kickoff for a game-winning TD. The Titans advanced to the franchise's first Super Bowl appearance.

# CHAPTER 5

# The BEST TEAMS in OTHER LEAGUES

Pro football isn't limited to the NFL. These teams also rule the gridiron

**PINBALL WIZARD**
Argonauts running back Michael (Pinball) Clemons (31) is the CFL's all-time leader in combined yards (25,438).

# CFL
### CANADIAN FOOTBALL LEAGUE
## Toronto Argonauts

Hockey may be Canada's official sport, but the country has a well-established football history too. The Canadian Football League started in 1958 and features a high-speed, high-scoring style of football. There is a lot of talent among the CFL's nine teams. Sometimes players do so well in the CFL that they make their way to the NFL. (The most famous example is Warren Moon, who won a CFL MVP award before becoming a nine-time Pro Bowler in the NFL.) No team has dominated the CFL more than the Toronto Argonauts. The Argos have won 17 Grey Cups—the CFL's equivalent to the Super Bowl. The most recent title was in 2017. They've benefited from legendary players like quarterback Doug Flutie, who went on to become an NFL star, and running back Michael (Pinball) Clemons, who holds the CFL career record for most combined yards (25,438).

**STAR BRIGHT**
The Philadelphia Stars won two of the three USFL championships behind QB Chuck Fusina.

# USFL

## UNITED STATES FOOTBALL LEAGUE
### Philadelphia Stars

The NFL has long been the most dominant professional football league, but for three seasons, there was a very active competitor. The United States Football League was launched in 1983 and was able to attract big-time talent, such as future Hall of Famers Jim Kelly, Steve Young, Reggie White, and Gary Zimmerman. Of the USFL's 18 teams, one stood above the rest. The Philadelphia Stars (who moved to Baltimore for the 1985 season) won a league-high 41 games and were USFL champions in two of the league's three seasons (1984 and 1985). The Stars were led by quarterback Chuck Fusina, who was named most outstanding quarterback and championship game MVP in 1984. Fusina threw for more than 10,000 yards and completed 66 touchdowns in his USFL career. The USFL would fold after the 1985 season, but many of its innovations, such as the two-point conversion and the coach's challenge, remain an important part of the game today.

**TD MACHINE**
Before becoming NFL MVP, Kurt Warner (13) threw 183 touchdowns in three seasons with the Barnstormers.

# AFL

## ARENA FOOTBALL LEAGUE
### *Iowa Barnstormers*

Nicknamed the War on the Floor, the Arena Football League became a quick success when it began in 1987. Played indoors, with no sidelines and with fans right on top of the action, the league was built for speed. The field is about a third of the size of an NFL field. Eight men play on a side, with many players lining up on defense and offense. The AFL puts a premium on passing, which made it perfect for Kurt Warner. After a failed NFL tryout in 1994 with the Packers, Warner joined the AFL's Iowa Barnstormers. With Warner, the Barnstormers played in two straight Arena Bowls, in 1997 and 1998. Warner would finish his three-season AFL career with 183 touchdowns. After he made the NFL, Warner threw 208 TDs in 11 NFL seasons. The AFL briefly closed in 2009 before returning in 2010. Currently, the league has four teams, all in the Northeast.

# WFL

WORLD FOOTBALL LEAGUE

## Birmingham Americans

The idea was to bring football to the world. Unfortunately, the farthest it got was Hawaii. The World Football League, launched in 1973, had a short run as a competitor to the NFL. The Toronto Northmen signed former Dolphins players Larry Csonka, Jim Kiick, and Paul Warfield to a combined $3.5 million deal, the richest in sports history at the time. But the league didn't last long enough for some deals to come to fruition. The World Football League played only one full season. In that 1974 season, the Birmingham Americans went 15–5, going undefeated in 13 home games, and won the championship. Quarterback George Mira, a veteran of three NFL teams, led Birmingham's offense, throwing for 2,248 yards and 17 touchdowns. He was also MVP of the championship game. The Americans wouldn't last past 1974, and the league itself only played 12 games in 1975 before closing. But the WFL did have a long-lasting impact. Five people associated with the league would become head coaches in the NFL.

# NFL EUROPE

NATIONAL FOOTBALL LEAGUE EUROPE

## Frankfurt Galaxy

In Europe, when you say "football," most people think about soccer. But for 16 seasons, the NFL brought the American version of the game to the continent. The World League of American Football—later shortened to NFL Europe—debuted in 1991 as a developmental league for aspiring NFL players. The league began with seven teams from the U.S. and Canada, along with one team each from Germany, England, and Spain. By 1995, the North American teams were disbanded, and the league expanded to include six European teams. The winner of that revamped 1995 season was Germany's Frankfurt Galaxy. Quarterback Paul Justin won World Bowl MVP honors after throwing three touchdowns in the Galaxy's 26–22 win over the Amsterdam Admirals from the Netherlands. In total, the Galaxy appeared in eight of the 15 World Bowls, winning four of them. Though NFL Europe shut down in 2007, it produced a number of quality NFL players, such as Kurt Warner, Adam Vinatieri, and Jake Delhomme.

**X MAN**
In 2001, Tommy Maddox (8) helped the Los Angeles Xtreme win the lone XFL title before leading the Pittsburgh Steelers to the NFL playoffs.

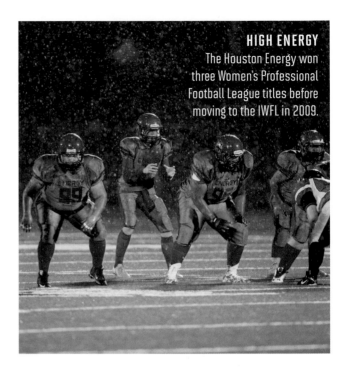

**HIGH ENERGY**
The Houston Energy won three Women's Professional Football League titles before moving to the IWFL in 2009.

# XFL

## Los Angeles Xtreme

For one season, in 2001, the XFL combined pro wrestling with football. The brainchild of WWE owner Vince McMahon, the XFL featured some unique rules. Instead of an opening coin toss, two players rushed toward midfield and wrestled for the ball, with the winner gaining possession. The XFL also allowed players to have nicknames on the backs of their jerseys. Running back Rod Smart became famous for wearing *He Hate Me* on his Las Vegas Outlaws jersey. The Los Angeles Xtreme won the lone XFL championship thanks in large part to quarterback Tommy Maddox. He led the league in passing yards and touchdowns and was the regular-season MVP. Maddox went straight from the XFL to the NFL, where he led the Pittsburgh Steelers to the playoffs in 2002. The original iteration of the XFL lasted only one season. But in 2018, McMahon announced plans to bring the XFL back in 2020.

# IWFL

### INDEPENDENT WOMEN'S FOOTBALL LEAGUE

## Houston Energy

Women have been playing football almost as long as men. In 1926, a women's team was the halftime entertainment for the Frankford Yellow Jackets (who later became the Philadelphia Eagles). Since then there have been a number of women's football leagues across the country. One constant has been the success of the Houston Energy. They started in the Women's Professional Football League and won three straight titles (2000–2002). In 2009, the Energy moved to the International Women's Football League, which had started in 2000. The team's winning ways continued. The Energy have since won two IWFL conference titles. Many IWFL players have other jobs but love the chance to be able to play the game they love. As Houston running back Stacey Agee, who scored three touchdowns in the Energy's first title game in 2000, once said, "I'd play for nothing."

# CHAPTER 6

# The G.O.A.T'S WITH THE MOST

Go inside the numbers with the NFL's best teams

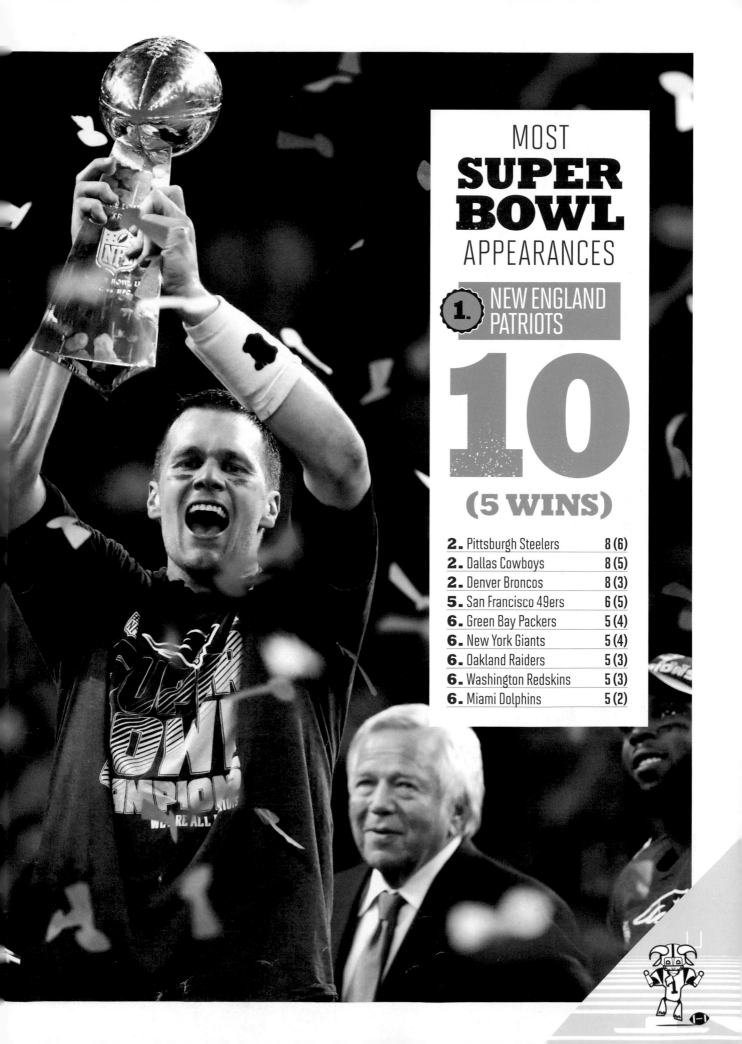

# MOST
# SUPER
# BOWL
## APPEARANCES

**1.** NEW ENGLAND PATRIOTS

# 10
## (5 WINS)

| | | |
|---|---|---|
| **2.** Pittsburgh Steelers | 8 (6) |
| **2.** Dallas Cowboys | 8 (5) |
| **2.** Denver Broncos | 8 (3) |
| **5.** San Francisco 49ers | 6 (5) |
| **6.** Green Bay Packers | 5 (4) |
| **6.** New York Giants | 5 (4) |
| **6.** Oakland Raiders | 5 (3) |
| **6.** Washington Redskins | 5 (3) |
| **6.** Miami Dolphins | 5 (2) |

# MOST WINS ALL TIME

**1.** CHICAGO BEARS

# 749

| | | |
|---|---|---|
| **2.** | Green Bay Packers | 737 |
| **3.** | New York Giants | 687 |
| **4.** | Pittsburgh Steelers | 614 |
| **5.** | Washington Redskins | 595 |
| **6.** | Philadelphia Eagles | 568 |
| **7.** | Los Angeles Rams | 555 |
| **8.** | Detroit Lions | 553 |
| **9.** | Arizona Cardinals | 550 |
| **10.** | San Francisco 49ers | 528 |

# MOST CONSECUTIVE WINS IN A SEASON

**1.** NEW ENGLAND PATRIOTS 2007

# 16

| | | |
|---|---|---|
| **2.** | Miami Dolphins, 1972 | 14 |
| **2.** | Pittsburgh Steelers, 2004 | 14 |
| **2.** | Indianapolis Colts, 2009 | 14 |
| **2.** | Carolina Panthers, 2015 | 14 |
| **6.** | Chicago Bears, 1934 | 13 |
| **6.** | Denver Broncos, 1998 | 13 |
| **6.** | Indianapolis Colts, 2005 | 13 |
| **6.** | New Orleans Saints, 2009 | 13 |
| **6.** | Green Bay Packers, 2011 | 13 |

## BEARS IN THE HALL OF FAME

DE Richard Dent

LB Dick Butkus

RB Walter Payton

LB Mike Singletary

RB Gale Sayers

TE Mike Ditka

# MOST HALL OF **FAMERS**\*

**1.** CHICAGO BEARS

# 34

|  |  | |
|---|------|---|
| **2.** | New York Giants | 31 |
| **3.** | Green Bay Packers | 30 |
| **3.** | Los Angeles Rams | 30 |
| **5.** | Washington Redskins | 29 |
| **6.** | Pittsburgh Steelers | 28 |
| **7.** | Oakland Raiders | 27 |
| **8.** | Philadelphia Eagles | 22 |
| **9.** | Cleveland Browns | 21 |
| **10.** | Detroit Lions | 20 |

\*Includes all teams that Hall of Famers played on

# MOST POINTS SCORED IN A **SEASON**

**1.** DENVER BRONCOS 2013

# 606

|  |  |  |
|---|------|--------|
| **2.** | New England Patriots, 2007 | 589 |
| **3.** | Green Bay Packers, 2011 | 560 |
| **4.** | New England Patriots, 2012 | 557 |
| **5.** | Minnesota Vikings, 1998 | 556 |
| **6.** | New Orleans Saints, 2011 | 547 |
| **7.** | St. Louis Rams, 2000 | 540 |
| **7.** | Atlanta Falcons, 2016 | 540 |
| **9.** | St. Louis Rams, 1999 | 526 |
| **10.** | Indianapolis Colts, 2004 | 522 |

## MOST PASSING TOUCHDOWNS IN A SEASON

**1.** DENVER BRONCOS 2013

# 55

| | | |
|---|---|---:|
| **2.** | Green Bay Packers, 2011 | 51 |
| **2.** | Indianapolis Colts, 2004 | 51 |
| **4.** | New England Patriots, 2007 | 50 |
| **5.** | Miami Dolphins, 1984 | 49 |
| **6.** | Houston Oilers, 1961 | 48 |
| **7.** | Miami Dolphins, 1986 | 46 |
| **7.** | New Orleans Saints, 2011 | 46 |
| **9.** | San Francisco 49ers, 1987 | 44 |
| **10.** | New Orleans Saints, 2012 | 43 |

QB Peyton Manning

## MOST FIRST DOWNS IN A SEASON

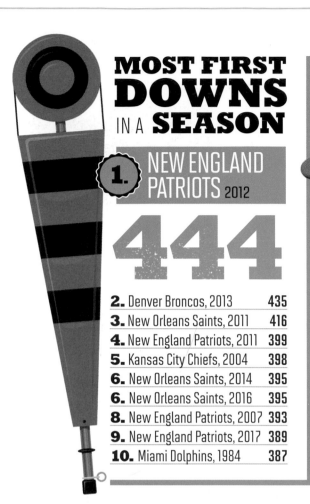

**1.** NEW ENGLAND PATRIOTS 2012

# 444

| | | |
|---|---|---:|
| **2.** | Denver Broncos, 2013 | 435 |
| **3.** | New Orleans Saints, 2011 | 416 |
| **4.** | New England Patriots, 2011 | 399 |
| **5.** | Kansas City Chiefs, 2004 | 398 |
| **6.** | New Orleans Saints, 2014 | 395 |
| **6.** | New Orleans Saints, 2016 | 395 |
| **8.** | New England Patriots, 2007 | 393 |
| **9.** | New England Patriots, 2017 | 389 |
| **10.** | Miami Dolphins, 1984 | 387 |

## MOST YARDS FROM SCRIMMAGE IN A SEASON

**1.** NEW ORLEANS SAINTS 2011

# 7,632

| | | |
|---|---|---:|
| **2.** | Denver Broncos, 2013 | 7,445 |
| **3.** | St. Louis Rams, 2000 | 7,335 |
| **4.** | Miami Dolphins, 1984 | 7,064 |
| **5.** | San Francisco 49ers, 1998 | 7,054 |
| **6.** | New England Patriots, 2012 | 7,028 |
| **7.** | New England Patriots, 2011 | 7,021 |
| **8.** | New Orleans Saints, 2016 | 7,000 |
| **9.** | Philadelphia Eagles, 2013 | 6,972 |
| **10.** | St. Louis Rams, 2001 | 6,930 |

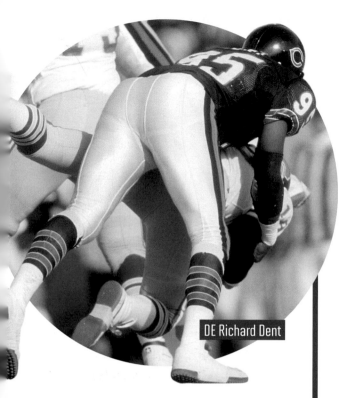

DE Richard Dent

# MOST INTERCEPTIONS
## IN A SEASON

**1.** SAN DIEGO CHARGERS 1961 **49**

| | | |
|---|---|---|
| **2.** | Green Bay Packers, 1943 | 42 |
| **3.** | New York Giants, 1951 | 41 |
| **4.** | Baltimore Colts, 1959 | 40 |
| **4.** | Green Bay Packers, 1940 | 40 |
| **4.** | New York Giants, 1933 | 40 |
| **7.** | New York Giants, 1948 | 39 |
| **7.** | San Francisco 49ers, 1986 | 39 |
| **9.** | Detroit Lions, 1953 | 38 |
| **9.** | Los Angeles Rams, 1952 | 38 |
| **9.** | Seattle Seahawks, 1984 | 38 |

# MOST SACKS*
## IN A SEASON

**1.** CHICAGO BEARS 1984 **72**

| | | |
|---|---|---|
| **2.** | Minnesota Vikings, 1989 | 71 |
| **3.** | Chicago Bears, 1987 | 70 |
| **4.** | New York Giants, 1985 | 68 |
| **5.** | Oakland Raiders, 1967 | 67 |
| **6.** | Boston Patriots, 1963 | 66 |
| **6.** | New Orleans Saints, 2000 | 66 |
| **6.** | New York Jets, 1981 | 66 |
| **6.** | Washington Redskins, 1984 | 66 |
| **10.** | Los Angeles Raiders, 1985 | 65 |

*Sacks became an official NFL stat in 1982.
Some teams kept their own records before that.

# MOST RUSHING TOUCHDOWNS
## IN A SEASON

**1.** GREEN BAY PACKERS 1962 **36**

FB Jim Taylor

| | | |
|---|---|---|
| **2.** | Pittsburgh Steelers, 1976 | 33 |
| **3.** | Kansas City Chiefs, 2003 | 32 |
| **3.** | San Diego Chargers, 2006 | 32 |
| **5.** | Kansas City Chiefs, 2004 | 31 |
| **6.** | Carolina Panthers, 2008 | 30 |
| **6.** | Chicago Bears, 1941 | 30 |
| **6.** | New England Patriots, 1978 | 30 |
| **6.** | Washington Redskins, 1983 | 30 |
| **10.** | Baltimore Colts, 1964 | 29 |
| **10.** | Seattle Seahawks, 2005 | 29 |

# INDEX

(Page numbers in bold refer to images.)

# PHOTO CREDITS